JOHNNY MACK BROWN

Up Close and Personal

by Bobby J. Copeland

Published by
Empire Publishing, Inc.
PO Box 717
Madison, NC 27025-0717

Phone: 336-427-5850 • Fax: 336-427-7372
Email: info@empirepublishinginc.com

Other books by Bobby J Copeland
Trail Talk, published by Empire Publishing
B-Western Boot Hill, published by Empire Publishing
Bill Elliott – the Peaceable Man, published by Empire Publishing
Roy Barcroft – King of the Badmen, published by Empire Publishing
Charlie King – We Called Him Blackie, published by Empire Publishing
Silent Hoofbeats, published by Empire Publishing.
The Bob Baker Story, published by BoJo Enterprises
The Whip Wilson Story, published by BoJo Enterprises
Five Heroes, published by BoJo Enterprises

Empire Publishing, Inc.
PO Box 717
Madison, NC 27025-0717
Phone: 336-427-5850
Fax: 336-427-7372
Email: info@empirepublishinginc.com

Library of Congress Control Number: 2005927406
ISBN Number: 978-0-944019-42-9

Published and printed inthe United States of America
1 2 3 4 5 6 7 8 9 10

COVER PHOTO by Jeffery Fain

DEDICATION

Dedicated to Cynthia Brown Hale (Johnny Mack's daughter), who provided me with many photos and the needed encouragement to go forward with the book.

SELECTED BIBLIOGRAPHIES

Anderson, Chuck, The Old Corral website.
Barbour, Alan*, The Thrill of it All*, (The McMillan Company, 1971).
Copeland, Bobby J., *The Bob Baker Story*, (BoJo Enterprises, 1998).
______, *B-Western Boot Hill*, (Empire Publishing, 1999).
______, *Trail Talk*, (Empire Publishing, 1996).
Cotterman, Don, article in *Horse and Rider* Magazine (unknown date)
Eames, John Douglas, *The MGM Story* (Crown, 1966).
Lodge, Stephen, *Behind the Scenes: Movies and Television* (unpublished).
McCord, Merrill, *Brothers of the West*, (Alhambra Publications, 2004).
Miller, Don*, Hollywood Corral*, (Popular Library Publishers, 1976).
O'Neal, Bill, *Tex Ritter—America's Most Beloved Cowboy*, (Eakin Press, 1998).
Parrish, James Robert & Stanke, Don, *Leading Ladies* (Arlington House, 1977).
Rainey, Buck, *The Strong Silent Type*, (McFarland & Company, 2004).
Rothel, David, *Those Great Cowboy Sidekicks*, (WOY Publications, 1984).
Russell, Bill, article in *The Old Cowboy Picture Show* (unknown date).
Thomas, Bob, *Joan Crawford* (Bantam Books, 1977).
Tuska, Jon, *The Filming of the West*, (Doubleday, 1976).
Wakely, Linda Lee*, See Ya Up There Baby! The Jimmy Wakely Story*, (Shasta Records, 1992).
Williams, Nick, article in *Western Film Collector* (unknown date).

Various issues of the following magazines:
Western Clippings
Western Revue
Modern Screen
Photo Play
The Motion Picture Herald

Special Thanks to the Following Individuals:

Boyd Magers
Richard B. Smith III
Paul Dellinger
John Brooker
Bob Tomko
Buck Rainey
Bill Russell
Doug Bruton
Mike Chew
Tinsley Yarbrough
Grady Franklin
Jim Hamby
Bill Sasser
Lois Hall
Bill Hale
Cynthia Brown Hale
Locky Brown
Joe Copeland
Lance Copeland
Lansing Sexton
Doug Morris
Mario DeMarco

TABLE OF CONTENTS

INTRODUCTION

Hollywood seemed to think that with enough publicity (much like the fabrications for Western stars such as Tom Mix, Ken Maynard and Whip Wilson), a handsome face, he-man physique, and the ability to at least sit on a horse, it could produce a Saturday matinee movie cowboy. But in the case of Johnny Mack Brown, Hollywood did not have to lend a hand—he already had more than the necessary requirements: he was handsome, a perfect physical specimen, a capable rider, and his exploits on the football field had provided him with plenty of publicity. In fact, if it had not for the publicity Brown had garnered on the gridiron, he would, in all likelihood, have never become a motion picture star and, even if he did, in all probability, his name would have been changed when he signed his movie contract. After all, John Brown was not a very catchy name for movie audiences.

THE EARLY YEARS

Johnny Mack Brown was born in Dothan (earlier called Poplar Head), Alabama, on September 1, 1904, the son of Hattie Estelle and John Henry Brown (Johnny's grandparents were John McGilvray 1845-1921, and Mary Ann Norton McGilvary 1846-1911. They are buried in Brundige, Alabama). Some two years earlier, Brown's parents were the talk of the town when they hustled off to get married.

The local newspaper, *The Troy Messenger*, reported the event: "Quite a stir was caused in the community last Sunday morning when it was noised abroad that a Gretna Green (school) affair had occurred the night before. Mr. J. H. Brown, of Banks, and Miss Hattie McGilvray, a pupil of the school, unmindful of parental objections, hid away to Bainbridge where they were married Sunday afternoon, reporting to Banks Monday morning.

Mr. Brown came down Saturday afternoon, and they had arranged to go on the south-

The house where Johnny Mack Brown was born stands at 519 S. St. Andrews St., Dothan, Alabama.

John Henry Brown and Hattie McGilvary (Johnny's parents).

bound 10:05 train, but the bride's brother appeared on the scene and was going to take her home. While he waited at the front door for her to get ready, she slipped out at the back door and joined her lover who was waiting nearby. They procured a conveyance and went to Tennille, where they took the first train to Bainbridge.

Mr. Brown is a well-known young businessman of Banks, where he has been a resident several years, gaining the respect of all who know him on account of his integrity of character. The young lady belongs to a family highly regarded in the Pronto neighborhood, having lived in that vicinity for a long period. She is intelligent, pretty and of a lovable disposition. She has hosts of friends who hope that she will be supremely happy throughout her married life. No blame can attach to the management of the school, for everyone knows 'Where there is a will, there is a way,' and 'Love laughs at locks and bars." (The marriage proved lasting – and fruitful; they had nine children, Harry, Johnny Mack, Tolbert, William "Billy" Wallace, Doris Fred, Louise, Elsa, David).

His mother once remarked about her adventuresome young Johnny, "I can recall that just about the time he was to enter the first grade school or a little before, the first automobile made its appearance in Dothan. This attracted him considerably and he was not content until he had thoroughly inspected this car. A friend of ours had purchased one of these cars and Johnny had learned where he kept it. Johnny Mack disappeared at lunch time, and a search was instituted. After several hours he was found in the improvised garage, dismantling the car bit by bit."

Johnny Mack Brown at the age of sixteen, when he was a football star on the Dothan High School team. This early gridiron fame led to his success later at the University of Alabama.

Brown developed an early love for the outdoors. He particularly enjoyed hunting and fishing and his love for these sports remained with him throughout his life. He described his early years, "We had a nice comfortable home, but it takes plenty of jack (money) to feed and clothe nine children. Dad wanted us to go to college, every one of us, but we knew that it would be up to us to help out with the expenses.

"I have the happiest memories of my childhood—fishing, hunting, swimming, picnics, social get-togethers, dancing, church meetings ... a montage of wonderful things I'll never forget, and, of course, football.

"In those days the high schools didn't have athletic budgets the way they have now, and we had to furnish a lot of our own equipment. We kids used to buy Boy Scout shoes and take them to a cobbler to have cleats put on. We played football on fields that looked like it was sewn with rocks.

"My father was a merchant in Dothan, but my spending money, or extras I wanted like a baseball mitt and so on I had to earn. To do this, I sold papers. One of the papers I sold was published by William Randolph Hearst. The first picture I made in Hollywood co-starred Marion Davies, Hearst's protégé. You never know how far a newspaper career will take you (laugh).

"Harry is the only one of us who was faithless to old Alabama. He went to Georgia Tech and was graduated there. That boy earned every penny of his way through school and was given highest honors. We are all mighty proud of Harry."

Not only was Johnny handsome and athletic, he was a fine dancer too. He never gave serious thoughts to dramatics in high school, but he did take part in at least two plays: "What Happened to Jones," and "Sprigg's Trip to Europe." He was an expert dancer, and played the mandolin and sang. These things, plus being a football star, made him very popular with the other students. Wallace Malone, a prominent banker told of an incident where he witnessed a tense rivalry football game between Johnny's team and Enterprise: "After the game there remained a great deal of bitter feelings. I felt the Enterprise boys were our guests and that they should be treated as such. When I reached the hotel, I heard an apologetic voice talking to our visitors. It was Johnny Mack Brown making an apology for the action of his teammates – all alone. It struck me as being a manly thing to do. When I heard next summer that Johnny was going to college, I realized it was quite a financial responsibility on his father, who had a large family to educate. I offered to lend him the necessary money until Johnny could secure a job. Johnny was a clean sportsman and a great moral boy, Dothan is proud of him, and he is proud of Dothan."

In his high school year book, *The Gargoyle*, his fellow classmates wrote of Brown, “We could write a book on his excellence and his shortcomings. We might write a paper, but we won’t write a solitary thing for everyone knows Johnny Mack. During athletic season, he’s the mainstay in more things than Eleanor’s swing – a jolly good fellow who is sure to star in the football world.” Johnny was voted the most handsome boy his last two years in high school.

Johnny’s high school graduation photo.

His high school teammate and quarterback, G. T. Cooper, said of Brown, “In Johnny Mack’s first year of football, he was a little slow in learning the plays. Instead of calling the signal for his play, I would have to tell him that I was going to give him the ball and wanted him to run like blazes with it. He became the best high school player who ever graduated from Dothan and possibly the best in the South. He was clumsy at first, but developed into the fastest man in Southern high school football at the time.”

Dothan High School football team. Johnny is on the center row, far right.

BROWN AT ALABAMA

(Auburn's loss is Alabama's gain)

Johnny had expressed an interest in attending college at Auburn University. He wanted to help the school defeat their hated rival, Georgia Tech. However, his parents wanted him to attend the University of Alabama. Near the time for Johnny to make a college decision, his mother became quite ill. Johnny visited her at the hospital and asked, "Mother is it really your wish for me to go to Alabama." She replied, "Yes, it is. I think you can do great things there." Immediately after leaving the hospital, he notified the University officials that he was coming to Alabama.

Brown said upon college arrival, "On the day of my 18th birthday I arrived at the University of Alabama. I can tell you I was green and scared and awed at all the buildings and the bigness—and loneliness. I was one of the first players in our part of the state to be named All-State, but I discovered when I got to the University that a lot of the All-State players had decided to go there.

"I thought I was a pretty good football player. When I went out for freshman football, I found the sledding tough. I weighed 139 pounds and discovered high school football quite different and the reputation gained there was hard to live up to. I barely made the squad as a frosh, but kept strict training and plugged away at the game."

Since Alabama had recruited a great class of football players, It took Johnny sometime to become a star. But he was anxious and eager to get on the field. He laughingly told of an incident during his sophomore season: "I am often reminded of the time we played the University of Syracuse. The University of Alabama was anything but a football power at that time. We were called the 'Thin Red Line.' But that was the first year of the coaching of Wallace Wade, and the 'Thin Red Line' was soon to surge forward as 'The Crimson Tide.'

"Coach Wade came to us from Vanderbilt University where he had been a professor and an assistant coach under Dan McGugin. About the first thing he did was to schedule a game with Syracuse, at the time one of the powerhouses of the East.

"We were mighty dismayed, but elated too. For many of us on the team it was our first trip out of state. And, for me and a few others, it was the first time in a sleeping car.

"The morning of the game they took us in limousines the 40 or 50 miles from where we had been staying to the Syracuse gym. It was the largest place I had ever seen, and we had the most luxurious dressing rooms we'd ever been in.

Then we looked around and saw stairs going down into a long tunnel. This came right up into the stadium.

"Well, things didn't go so well for us. That was my sophomore year and it was early in the season, and I hadn't made the team yet as a regular. But we weren't far into the game when Coach Wade told me to warm up. I jumped up and raced up and down the sidelines behind the bench. The Syracuse co-eds were sitting right behind us, exchanging cheers with the men students across the field. I would run until I got tired and then I'd stop by the coach, panting. In a while he'd notice me and say, 'Brown, warm up.' And I'd go back running up and down. I did that the entire first half. Then, when the second half started, my warming up started all over again. Finally, it was obvious to everyone that we were in too much of a hole to get out. The co-eds behind us took up a new chant, 'Put the race-horse in,' they yelled. 'Put the racehorse in.' I never did get in that game, but I was as tired as if I'd played 60 minutes.

"In 1924 I was a junior on the team that beat Georgia Tech for the first time in five years, 14-0. The next year, during our last game, I caught a punt and ran it back for a touchdown against them. We beat them 7-0 and went to the Rose Bowl to play the University of Washington. Connie was in the official party as a sponsor. We had been going together for three years and we were married the following June.

"The rest of those years are now part of a glorious history as Mr. Wade's coaching began to take effect. I remember some of the things he used to say to us: 'A good football player never gets hurt.' That kept us on our toes. And, 'It always takes that extra effort to make a touchdown.' Also, 'Anybody can go when he's feeling good; but the man I want is the one who, when he is tired, can still go.'

"Most everybody, who remembers those days at the University, knew Pooley Hubert, one of the best quarterbacks Alabama ever had. Pooley was several years older than me. It was custom in those days for the 'old men' of the fraternities to raid other houses when they could and beat up the 'rats' – the freshmen. I was alone at Kappa Sigma house one day when the KA's (one the fraternities) came streaming in through the door and some of the windows. I beat them up the stairways and onto the sleeping porch, where I remembered there was a trap door in the ceiling to the attic. I got up on one those two-tiered beds and into the trap door just as Pooley grabbed my leg. I shook him off, closed the door, put a mattress down, and went to sleep. That was the end of that."

During the summers, Johnny worked at the Charles Black Company, a smart haberdashery, for $25.00 a month. Lee Black, the proprietor of the store, said "Johnny was very popular with the ladies and every time one would enter the store, she would ask for Johnny Mack."

The football game that changed the South

(Courtesy of the *University of Alabama Center for Public Television and Radio*)

It was more than a football game. It was the chance to avenge the South, to reclaim the valor and honor of the Lost Cause. No longer would this land be known for its hookworm and illiteracy. It would be the home of the best damn football in the nation!

"The 1926 Rose Bowl was without a doubt the most important game before or since in Southern football history," says Birmingham News sportswriter Clyde Bolton. "For the first time in 50 years of college football, the game was dominated by powerhouses in the North, Midwest, and West – Princeton, Yale, Harvard, Washington, and others. Southern boys can't compete, the experts said. In fact, the prevailing sentiment was that the South wasn't good for much of anything." "H.L. Mencken at the Baltimore Sun was writing very critical and satiric editorials about the brain cavity size of the typical Southerner and it was not at all uplifting or complimentary to the South," said Wayne Flynt, history professor at Auburn University.

But in 1925 the University of Alabama had its first undefeated season and gave up only seven points. Still, no Southern team—Alabama included—had earned enough respect to get an invitation to the Rose Bowl in Pasadena.

Schools back east, reeling from criticism that they were sacrificing academics at the expense of athletics, declined to play in the game. So bowl officials reluctantly booked a game everyone knew would be a blow-out—a weak Alabama team against the mighty Washington Huskies.

"Roses of Crimson" (a video) shows how the team made its way west on a four day train trip while dealing poker and studying their playbooks. Once in California, Alabama coach Wallace Wade feared that his team was being distracted by the photo opportunities that had been arranged by Hollywood press moguls. So he sequestered his players and put them through some of the toughest practices of the season.

Meanwhile, Champ Pickens, a tireless Alabama promoter, began predicting an upset and constantly reminded the players about their obligation to history. He wired all the presidents of the civic clubs in Tuscaloosa and told them to send telegrams out to the Alabama players that the honor of the Confederacy was on their shoulders. They had to avenge losing the Civil War by beating these Washington Yankees," Bolton explained. No matter that the Yankees in the state of Washington had nothing to do with the South's defeat in 1865. Even Wade played on loyalty to the region, when Alabama went into the locker room at the half trailing 12-0. "And they told me Southern boys would fight," was all he told his team.

In the second half the unbelievable happened. Quarterback Pooley Hubert, the seasoned and mature team leader, kept running straight into the Washington line until he scored. Johnny Mack Brown, the dashing running back who would become a matinee movie idol, caught a fifty-yard pass in full stride and made a touchdown.

Everyone at the Rose Bowl was stunned. Hubert sensed Alabama could deliver a knockout blow and called an audacious play. "Pooley told me to run up field as fast as I could," recalled Brown. "When I reached the three-yard line, I looked back and sure enough the ball was coming over my shoulder. I took it in stride and went over carrying somebody. The place was really in an uproar."

"Roses of Crimson" shows how the uproar continued after the game. In nearly every town the team's train passed through on the trip back to Tuscaloosa, Southerners struck up brass bands and hailed the conquering heroes. In New Orleans, nearly one thousand Tulane students rallied when the train pulled into the station. And back at the University of Alabama campus, the entire student body and most of the town turned out for a raucous parade that ended with speeches and tributes on the Quad.

"The documentary has some wonderful scenes from a great game, but it's about more than that," said Tom Rieland, who produced the documentary for The University of Alabama Center for Public Television and Radio. 'It also shows why Southerners were ready for something that would unite them that would give them a reason to say they were proud to be from Dixie – this football game did that."

Now it's hard to imagine a time in the South when a Monday post-mortem of the game didn't dominate conversation at the office water-cooler, or when weekend events in the fall didn't revolve around attending a game or at least watching one on TV.

"You can look at the 1926 Rose Bowl as the most significant event in Southern football history," said Andrew Doyle, a history professor at Winthrop University who has written about the sport. "What had come before was almost like a buildup, a preparation for this grand coming out party. And it was a sublime tonic for Southerners who were buffeted by a legacy of defeat, military defeat, a legacy of poverty, and a legacy of isolation from the American political and cultural mainstream."

Charles "The Durango Kid" Starrett told an interesting story at the 1984 Raleigh Film Festival regarding the 1926 Rose Bowl, "I played for Dartmouth and we were invited to play in the Rose Bowl that year. At that time, the Ivy League schools did not look favorably upon participating in bowl games, so Dartmouth turned down the invitation and it was extended to Alabama. If my team had accepted the invitation to play in the game, Johnny wouldn't have got the opportunity to shine in the Rose Bowl, and may have never become a Western picture star. I used to kid him by saying, 'If it had not been for Dartmouth's refusal to play in the game, you may have ended up coaching football somewhere in Alabama.'"

University of Alabama Football Hall of Fame

(Publicity statement issued by the Alabama Athletic Department at the time of Johnny's induction to the Hall.)

Johnny Mac (sic) *Brown*: A *two time Southern Conference player, Brown is best remembered for his role in Alabama's win over Washington in the 1926 Rose Bowl.*

Inducted into the Collegiate Hall of Fame in 1957, his performance in that '26 Rose Bowl earned him a spot on the all-time Rose Bowl team. Known as the "Dothan Antelope" during his playing days, he was the first of four brothers to play for Tide. He died of kidney disease November 15 (sic), 1974, in California.

(Author's Note: The University should have done a better job of research. Not only was the "k" left out of Mack, his death date was November 14.)

Letter from the College Football Hall of Fame

Johnny Mack Brown is remembered as perhaps the first athlete who successfully pursued a motion picture career. As a football player at the University of Alabama, Brown played in one of the most important games in Southern football history.

Until Alabama defeated Washington 20-19 in the 1926 Rose Bowl, Southern football did not enjoy the prestige it holds today. The 1926 Rose Bowl provided the first opportunity for Southern football to gain national recognition. Trailing 12-0 at halftime, Alabama changed its offensive strategy to utilize Brown's pass catching ability. In the third quarter, Brown was on the receiving end of a 61-yard and a 38-yard touchdown pass play. Alabama won the game. Alabama posted a 10-0 record while shutting out eight opponents.

Brown's play in the Rose Bowl inspired the game's head linesman to say, "Johnny Mack Brown has the sweetest feet I have ever seen. The way he managed to elude Washington tacklers in his long runs was marvelous. He has a weaving elusive style that is beautiful to watch." The game's referee, Walter J. Eckersall, said, "No player ever delighted a football crowd in history as Johnny Mack Brown, of Alabama, in the Rose Bowl New Year's Day, 1926."

Of course, Johnny was named the game's most valuable player for the Alabama side. George Wilson won the honor for Washington. Despite many calling Brown's performance "one of the greatest in the Rose Bowl's history," George Wilson was elected to the Bowl's Hall of Fame some ten years prior to Brown's selection.

Like many, Johnny's son Lachlan, was puzzled as to why it had taken so long for the Hall to honor his father and commented, "I was surprised to learn there was a Rose Bowl Hall of Fame when they contacted me. I asked how long it had been in existence and when advised, my first thought was 'and you are just now getting around to dad?' Then while perusing the photos, after the presentation luncheon, I noticed that George Wilson had already been inducted, I again was surprised."

Article from the State of Alabama Sports Hall of Fame

(Author's Note: Although some of this has been mentioned earlier I thought it important to include all of the following article from the State of Alabama's first Sports Hall of Fame program (1969) when Brown along with seven others including Paul "Bear" Bryant, Joe Louis, and Don Hutson were inducted.)

It was Jan. 1, 1926, Alabama was playing Washington in the Rose Bowl, with much more at stake than the winning or losing of a football game. This was the testing time for Southern football. The Crimson Tide was blazing a trail, the first team from the South to appear on the West Coast.

It was generally acknowledged that the East and West Coast formed the power structure of college football. It was up to Alabama to crash the establishment. The prestige of Dixie was on the line, finally do or die.

Alabama quickly dropped two touchdowns behind. A rout appeared imminent. Washington carried its 12-0 lead into the third quarter. If Alabama would strike a blow for the South it had to be now. The quick Southerners of Wallace Wade did strike, with lightning fury. A ground assault produced one touchdown, and Tide confidence lifted as the score became 12-7.

From this point, the blazing speed and clever running of Johnny Mack Brown carried the Crimson Tide to glory. Brown, labeled "The Dothan Antelope" by Southern sportswriters, put on a show many still call the greatest in Rose Bowl history. He first got behind Washington's secondary and took a 63-yard scoring pass from Grant Gillis. It put Alabama ahead to stay.

But the handsome lad from Dothan wasn't through. When the Tide recovered a fumble shortly after the kickoff, Johnny Mack was ready to burn the Huskies again. He again sped away from Washington's secondary, grabbed Pooley Hubert's well-aimed pass and scored his second touchdown. Alabama missed the extra point, but that was of little consequence—Washington was beaten, done in by the flying feet of Johnny Mack Brown. The South had established its place in the football sun.

That game, more than any other, launched a tradition Alabama football enjoys to this day. And Johnny Mack Brown, as much as any player, is responsible. That's why the man from Dothan's Wiregrass, who went on to fame as a Western movie hero, is being installed as a charter member of Alabama's Sports Hall of Fame.

Brown's brilliance in the Rose Bowl was no fluke. He played three magnificent years at Alabama, and was the key man during a period that saw the Tide win 25, lose three and tie one. Johnny Mack was All-Southern halfback/safety in 1924 and 1925.

There were many big moments in the football career of Alabama's star halfback. One of the biggest, which kept Alabama undefeated en route to the Rose Bowl, was Johnny Mack's 55-yard punt return to beat Georgia Tech, 7-0, in Atlanta the year before, when Alabama became the first Southern team to defeat Georgia Tech under Coach Bill Alexander. Brown caught a 37-yard touchdown pass and gained 135 yards in 10 rushes. The Tide won that one 14-0.

Other highlights of Johnny Mack's playing days were a three-touchdown performance in the opening game of 1924, a 55-0 rout of Union; a 99-yard kickoff return against Kentucky the same year; a 79-yard punt return and two touchdown day against Kentucky in 1925; and two touchdowns on passes from Hubert against Florida later in the season.

During his three years, Brown scored at least 15 touchdowns, details of some games being rather spotty. Most were on long runs and pass receptions. Coach Hank Crisp, assistant on Wade's staff, who stayed active in

University athletics more than 45 years, says of the Dothan speedster, "Johnny Mack is the best runner I have seen at Alabama. I don't know what kind of step it was, but he could jump sideways and still not lose forward speed. One man wasn't going to hem him up,"

Following his playing days, which ended with the memorable Rose Bowl, Johnny Mack returned to the University. He was a student coach on Wade's staff during the 1926 season. When Alabama returned to the Rose Bowl in 1927, he went along and it was at that time Johnny Mack got his start in the movies. Contrary to popular legend, it wasn't the Rose Bowl game that brought him to films. Earlier, Johnny Mack became acquainted with George Fawcett on a film location in Alabama. Fawcett urged the handsome young football player to try films. During the 1927 trip Johnny Mack looked up Fawcett, who showed him around the studios. A contract with MGM followed. Brown played his first Western role with a flapper named Joan Crawford. He later played romantic roles opposite Greta Garbo, Marion Davies and Norma Shearer, and co-starred with Mary Pickford in COQUETTE, which won her an Academy Award. Johnny Mack specialized in Westerns at Universal and later at Monogram, where he ground out 7 movies a year.

The all-time Alabama great was enshrined in the National Football Hall of Fame in 1957, one of six Crimson Tiders to be so honored. Formal induction was made at the homecoming game against Mississippi State, October 26 that year. The inscription on the Hall of Fame plaque reads: "Johnny Mack Brown has been granted the highest honors of the National Football Hall of Fame in recognition of his playing ability as demonstrated in intercollegiate competition, his sportsmanship, integrity, character and contributions to the sport of football. This certificate bears witness that his name shall be forever honored in the National Football Hall of Fame"

Johnny meets Cornelia

Johnny told about meeting the strikingly beautiful Cornelia "Connie" Bacon Foster: "I almost didn't meet her. I keep thanking my lucky stars that my roommate at the University of Alabama did a bit of bragging about his date for the Kappa Sigma tea dance that autumn afternoon. I hadn't planned to go to the dance, but he kept raving about his date until my curiosity was aroused. I drifted down and stood at the edge of the dance floor, watching the couples dance around to a favorite tune of mine. 'Here she is, Johnny Mack,' I heard my friend say, and turned to greet him. Beside him stood a slim, dark girl; she was about 18. She had a fascinating smile that made you want to smile back. 'Cornelia Foster,' he said, 'this is Johnny Mack Brown. Johnny Mack—Cornelia, Judge Henry Bacon Foster's daughter.'

"'Everybody knows Alabama's star halfback,' she laughed. 'No introductions are necessary. I've been watching you play all season.'

"I started thanking providence for the fellow who invented football. I kept thinking, 'What if I hadn't come this afternoon. What if I hadn't met her?' I knew this was a pretty important moment in my life.

"Cornelia Foster was the embodiment of all I'd ever dreamed a woman could be. She was quite tall, about 5-6. She had huge dark-brown eyes and dark hair, cut short and close, but sort of fluffy around her face. She was the loveliest girl I had ever seen. I managed to come out of my trance and ask her to dance with me at last. We seemed to know from the first we were meant for each other. I took her to fraternity dances and school proms, and pretty soon Cornelia wore my fraternity pin over her heart.

"New Year's Day that year found our football team in the Pasadena Rose Bowl, fighting the University of Washington for the Bowl championship. It was a school tradition to take along co-ed sponsors when the team made long trips to championship games, and Cornelia accompanied us as one of them.

"On the train there was a lot of noise and fun. A huge number of Alabama fans had come along with us. The car was packed with people singing school songs, laughing and celebrating. Cornelia and I were sitting there, singing sometimes, mostly just talking. I asked her to marry me. She grinned that cute, lovely, grin of hers and said, 'Wait until after the game, and I'll give you my answer. And you'd better going!' 'Is that a bribe?' I asked. She nodded, laughing.

"We won by the skin of our teeth, beating Washington 20-19. That was a wild, exciting day. The Bowl was packed full of rabid fans. They crowded out on the field like mad the minute the final gun sounded. "Cornelia came running out across the field to me and threw her arms around my neck, excitedly kissing me and laughing. I held her close a minute, listening to her laugh against my cheek. 'If you hadn't won,' she was saying her big dark eyes full of mischief, 'the answer would still have been yes.'

"If you've ever seen a happy guy, I was one. A Rose Bowl championship and a 'yes' from the girl I loved both on the same day!"

He and Connie were married at her home in Tuscaloosa, Alabama, on June 9, 1926. Johnny was selling insurance for the Aetna Life Insurance Company at the time.

Although he often expressed love for the University of Alabama, and is in the University's Hall of Fame, he did not get a diploma from the school.

Johnny expresses his love for his home state

"It would be difficult for me to express enough gratitude or to show enough appreciation for all the help, love and happy memories I have of Alabama and my hometown, Dothan—and for the many fine people who have been so kind to me throughout the years. Friends and friendships crowd in upon my memory. I wish I could talk about all of them.

"When I was a boy growing up in Dothan, and through my schoolhood and university days, I had wonderful times. Alabama will always be home and, in everything I've done, I have wanted the folks there to be proud of me.

"One of my biggest thrills was going home after the Rose bowl game. As the train pulled into Dothan, there was a big crowd to meet it, and I looked out the window and saw my brother playing trap drums with the band. They gave me one of the finest receptions anyone could ever wish for. There was a luncheon at the hotel with my mother and daddy there, and speeches, speeches, speeches.

"My home state has treated me more than royally on many occasions. There was the Peanut Festival in Dothan when I was grand marshal of the festivities...and the time Birmingham proclaimed Johnny Mack Brown Day during the Fat Stock Show and Rodeo. A person doesn't forget things like that easily ... you can't beat Alabama folks, or ever hope for better friends."

At football practice at Alabama.

National Football Hall of Fame

John Mack Brown
University of Alabama
All America Back, 1924-1925

has been granted the highest honors of the National Football Hall of Fame, in recognition of his outstanding playing ability as demonstrated in intercollegiate competition, his sportsmanship, integrity, character, and contribution to the sport of football, this certificate bears witness that his name shall be forever honored in the
National Football Hall of Fame

Elected:
February 20, 1957
New Brunswick, N.J.

Bill Cunningham
Chairman, Honors Court

Johnny carries the football against Washington in the Rose Bowl game.

Football Hall of Fame ceremony.

HOLLYWOOD BECKONS

Character actor George Fawcett, and some other actors, were invited to an Alabama football game while they were in the State to film MEN OF STEEL, when he noticed the handsome Brown. It was Fawcett who suggested to Johnny that he should try to get in the movies. Fawcett said of the meeting, "It was in Birmingham, and Johnny had been the star performer for Alabama.

"After the game, Johnny was brought over to meet us actors. I said to him, 'You ought to come to Hollywood, son, and have a try at pictures' 'Why thanks,' he stammered, 'that's awfully nice of you, but I'm not an actor. Gee, I'd be scared to death out there. You don't need me. All I can do is run around with a pigskin.'"

Johnny recalled the incident, "The game was 'on ice' because we had run up a good score against Vanderbilt. The coach pulled me out. That's when Fawcett suggested that I have a screen test. But he wasn't actually a talent scout because he was one of the stars of that picture they were making there."

Sometime after the talk with Fawcett, Brown decided to give Hollywood a try.

He was contacted by a motion picture scout named Champ Pickens and a screen test was arranged. Johnny and his Connie stayed at the Fawcett estate while waiting on the screen test results.

Brown had photographed well and was offered a contract by MGM, one of Hollywood's biggest studios. After just a few small roles at MGM, he became a star during the waning days of silent films.

Connie told of Johnny's first encounter with Hollywood, "I think his first contract with at MGM started at $75.00 a week. It increased at the option times during the four and one half years he was at MGM. When he left the studio, he was an established leading man and could demand higher prices while free-lancing at other studios. When talkies came he, like most actors, took voice and singing lessons." Connie went on to say, "We spent many Sundays at the beach home of Marion Davies and her friend William Randolph Hearst. Johnny was also a winner at one of Davies' costume party – dressed as an Indian."

The friendship between George Fawcett and John Mack Brown started at a football game in Alabama. Fawcett advised the athlete to go to Hollywood. When Brown arrived, Fawcett spent his evenings training him for his new career.

(Author's Note: I believe Connie's statement regarding her and Johnny's friendship with Hearst and Davies should put to rest the rumors about Johnny having an affair with Davies, and the claim that Hearst had Johnny black-balled at the major Hollywood studios).

Connie continued, "I knew Johnny Mack would not do his best work if I'm sitting on the set, watching him. It would be embarrassing and difficult for the girl he is playing opposite to know his wife is present." However, Connie was not above offering advice to Johnny about his love scenes: "Why, Johnny Mack," she would say, with that southern drawl, when they would come back from a preview of one of his pictures, "You ought to be ashamed of yourself, sure enough. You know how to kiss a girl better than that. Why didn't you kiss her like you meant it – this way?" Then she proceeded to give him a big kiss to show him what she meant.

Connie was asked which thrilled her most – Johnny's football days or his pictures: "That's a rather difficult question. Of course I love football. I think the biggest thrill was when Alabama was playing Kentucky and Johnny Mack caught the ball two yards behind the goal and ran 102 yards for a touchdown. The crowd was yelling and cheering like wild Indians and it seemed like something inside me would simply burst with excitement. I guess that will be one of the things I'll remember—always. Then I think my biggest screen thrill was when Johnny Mack played opposite Mary Pickford in COQUETTE. But it was the sort of thrill that put a lump in my throat. I guess the football thrill was physical and the other more aesthetic."

A critic praised Johnny for his work in the 1928 MGM entry, SQUARE CROOKS: "John Mack Brown is effectively natural." While at MGM, Johnny worked with some of the movie industry's legendary female stars, such as Mary Pickford, Joan Crawford, Greta Garbo, Mae West, and Norma Shearer. Brown emerged as a leading man, usually billed as John Mack Brown. He was also loaned out to other studios such as Paramount, Fox and RKO during this period. Although he is today best known for his Westerns, most of his silent films were dramas and comedies.

With the advent, and studio acceptance, of synch-sound pictures, Brown's star began to fade at MGM, as studio executives thought his strong southern accent was not becoming of a leading man. However, the accent proved to be an asset in Westerns with the October 1930 release of BILLY THE KID, in which Brown had the title role. He had appeared earlier that year in the semi-Western MONTANA MOON, with Joan Crawford. The picture was a real dud and bombed at the box-office. Prior to BILLY THE KID, he had been billed as John Mack Brown, but in this film, he was billed as Johnny Mack Brown. Destiny had its way with the making of BILLY THE KID. The picture co-starred Wallace Beery as lawman Pat Garrett and, for the sake of authenticity, was partly filmed, around Gallup, New Mexico. It is significant that this was a Western story and that it was successful because it was the first time Brown had really had the chance to swap pigskin for buckskin to finally give the public a look at him in a cowboy setting. They looked, and they loved it.

Strangely enough King Vidor, who directed the picture, objected to the casting of Johnny as "Billy the Kid," claiming he looked more like a varsity athlete than a ruthless young outlaw. Author Hal Erickson seemed to agree with Vidor and wrote the following for *The All Movie Guide*:

> *"The tall and virile Johnny Mack Brown portrays the short and dyspeptic outlaw William Bonney a.k.a. Billy the Kid. Wallace Beery is more effectively cast as Pat Garrett the sheriff who's sworn to bring in Billy dead or alive despite his grudging friendship for the young killer. Hardly the 'homicidal moron' described by Western historians, the movie's Billy has a certain amount of charm, though he's shown to be a cold-blooded killer when the opportunity arises.*
>
> *The film's ending was shot twice: One ending retained fidelity to the facts by having Garrett kill Billy, while the other allowed Billy to ride into the sunset, as Garrett beatifically looked on. Over the protests of western purists, the second ending was used in the American release version, though the more tragic climax was seen by European audiences. BILLY THE KID*

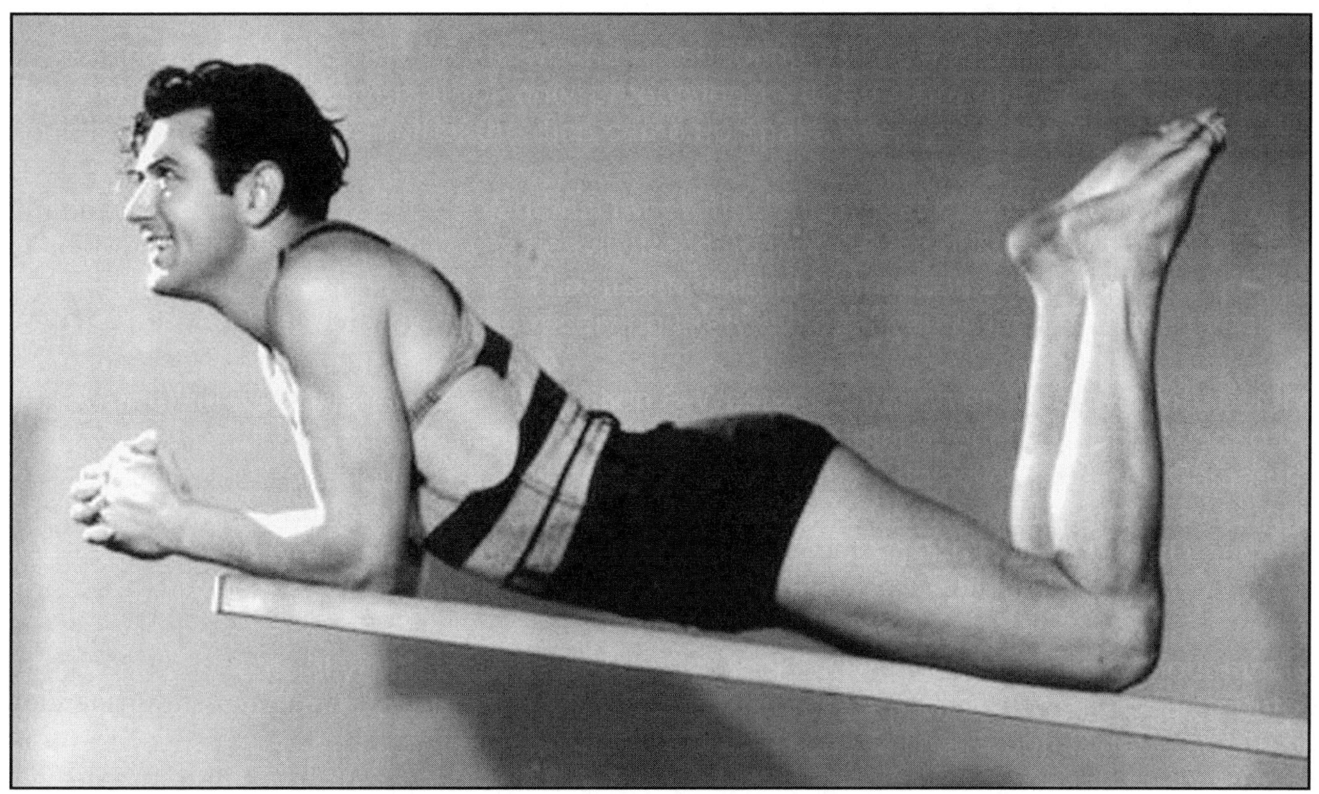

Johnny displays the latest men's swimwear in a publicity still (circa 1928).

An interesting group at John Mack Brown's tennis party. From left to right: Lew Ayres, Ginger Rogers, Virginia Valli and her husband Charles Farrell, Fay Wray, and Barbara Weeks.

> *was originally released in a 70mm widescreen process called Realife; to avoid confusion with MGM's 1941 BILLY THE KID, the earlier film has been retitled "The Highwayman Rides" for television.*

Another critic praised Johnny's performance: *Johnny Mack Brown does the show of his life as the boy outlaw. Not history. But who wants history. The movie's a pip.*

Brown was thrilled to play the role and said, "Every boy who ever lived has played a bandit at some time in his life, and every boy who ever lived read all the adventure stories he could find. It's just human nature, I reckon, for us to like to hear about folks who do things we wouldn't dare to do or wouldn't want to do. That's why I was so tickled when they gave me the part of Billy. He's sort of a mixture of all the two-gun characters that Harry and Tolbert (his brothers) and I used to read about. And best of all, he's a real person, not imaginary one. It was the biggest kick of my life to go to the country where he actually lived, making scenes for the picture, and to listen to the old settlers who really knew Billy. I felt as if I was living in a paper-backed thriller!"

Johnny with his hot new Oldsmobile.

He also told of William S. Hart being advisor on the film: "Bill and I became great friends. He gave me autographed copies of some of the books he had written. He taught me a great many things—how to crouch, for instance, and turn your left side away, to protect your heart. He told me to diminish your target and keep your heart as far away as you can from an enemy's bullet. I followed his advice when I had a gun battle in a picture. Bill gave me one of Billy the Kid's guns; I still have it."

Despite the huge pre-release publicity, money spent, and directing of King Vidor, BILLY THE KID, like John Wayne's first large-scale Western, THE BIG TRAIL, was a box

Johnny at Paramount (circa 1929).

Johnny with Lane Chandler (MGM, 1929).

office disappointment. One reason for the lack of success was because both films were shot in 70mm and many of the theaters were not equipped to show this type of film. Also, the pictures were made during the Great Depression and people had little money to spend on entertainment.

Don Miller, in his excellent book *Hollywood Corral,* compared the careers of Brown and Wayne: "You might say the career of Johnny Mack Brown is what John Wayne's would have been, if STAGECOACH hadn't happened. Perhaps, in cold print it looks like a putdown, which it certainly isn't meant to be. In truth, Brown's Western career began with a big splash, as did Wayne's, and both their films were unsuccessful, or disappointing, at the box-office. Thereafter, they floundered somewhat. In the dramatic roles, they seemed stiff and uncomfortable and both gradually drifted into low-budget Westerns to attain some measure of popularity. Where Wayne carved a trail to fame, Brown became a durable cowboy star, starring at the same time as Charles Starrett with a Western series rivaling the Columbia player for length of service, though not for one studio. If Wayne's screen work was more concentrated on the Western form, then Brown's films experience surely ranged wider in a variety of roles. If Wayne hit meteoric heights, Brown's coterie of well-wishers was no less rabid."

The December 1931 issue of *The New Movie Magazine* had a small blurb about Brown: "Johnny Mack Brown will not be at a loss for someone to talk football to, now that Weldon Heyburn has arrived in Hollywood. Johnny and Weldon were roommates at the University of Alabama and both played football – and how!"

Apparently the Heyburn story was only Hollywood-hype because when Kenneth Gaddy, director of the Paul W. Bryant Museum in Alabama, was contacted, he issued the following statement: "We can not find Weldon Heyburn listed as a player or even a student at Alabama. He is neither on the letterman list nor in the University yearbooks."

The handsome Heyburn appeared as a "dress" heavy in several B-Westerns with such cowboy greats as George O'Brien, William Boyd, Gene Autry, Roy Rogers, Sunset Carson, Charles Starrett, and Bill Elliott – but he never made a picture with Johnny.

MGM had not forgotten Johnny, and the studio briefly considered him for the role of TARZAN THE APEMAN (1932). Strangely enough, only a few years later (1939), Johnny's son, Lachlan, auditioned for the role of Tarzan's son for TARZAN FINDS A SON.

Lachlan Brown recalled the interview: "It did happen. I went to the studio, in hand with dad, in a yellow, short pant, sun suit—the kind with shoulder straps and a bib-like front. I was probably five. I sat in a small room and someone came in after a while and interviewed me. Basically what I recall of the interview was him asking me if I could swim and of course I answered a resounding – 'yes.' I loved the water and learned to swim early. He also asked me if I could swim underwater which again I said 'yes,' to that he asked how far underwater. I pointed to the opposite wall in the room and said – 'over there.' I have no idea how far that was and when you are small all rooms look large, but I do recall that room didn't appear large. But to the other wall was a good distance for a five year old. That really is all I recall of the interview. I have always wondered how I ended up going on that interview, though I never thought to ask Mom or Dad. I did learn later that the kid (Johnny Sheffield) who got the part had previous stage experience.

"Several years later, while in the Cub Scouts, I went to a Scout conclave in the Malibu area and, during the ceremonies, Johnny Sheffield was introduced as one of the Cub Scouts there and they made a big deal over him. Despite my complete lack of interest and concern over not being selected, that attention sort of irritated me, but it did pass quickly. Its funny how certain things stick in your memory."

Johnny and Connie win the costume contest at Marion Davies.

Johnny and friend and fellow actor, William Bakewell, celebrate by jumping the net after a game of tennis.

A publicity shot of Johnny. The studio straightened his hair and doctored his eyebrows (circa 1929).

Johnny in his dude clothes.

Johnny in another of his dude outfits (from an unknown magazine circa 1929).

THE HOLLYWOOD MANSION

It was during the early 1930s when Johnny and his wife Connie became part of the "Hollywood society." They purchased a home in Beverly Hills which included all the amenities expected for the Hollywood elite. Their friends included some of Hollywood's biggest names such as Jeanette McDonald, Mary Pickford, Douglas Fairbanks, Spencer Tracy and many more.

On June 16, 1937, a California newspaper had a photo of the wedding of Jeanette

Johnny and Connie on the porch of their English mansion (circa 1936).

McDonald and Gene Rayborn, and Johnny and Connie were in the photo – along with several Hollywood dignitaries. Connie was one of the bridesmaids at the wedding.

Locky, Cynthia, Beau, a dog, Janie, Sally, Connie, and Johnny in the "drawing room." (circa 1949).

Johnny told about his family, and house (circa 1948): "For quite some time now, as a member of the Hollywood sage-brush set, I've been heading the posse beating back the rustlers, redeeming the ranch and saving the little gal. And as far as I'm concerned, I intend to keep right on doing it until Brown and his hoss, Rebel, both trips over their beards.

"I'm mighty proud that the Western picture provides its own particular brand of entertainment for Mr. and Mrs. Moviegoer. I'm proud because the plots of Western pictures are basic and honest, woven of the sturdy stuff of high morals and honesty—and I like knowing that there are millions of people who advocate and admire those principles. I like the letters that I receive from all over the world—packs of them from England—stating that fans never go away from Western pictures disappointed.

Johnny and daughter Jane ready for a tennis match (circa 1949).

"The Western star can't disappoint his friends in any other department either. The public thinks of him off-screen as the same tireless, honest individual he portrays as Western hero. And he'd better maintain that standard in his private life! I think it wouldn't hurt a bit if every person in the public eye, politician or actor, felt a little of the same rigid responsibility. A Western actor knows he's through if he fails the people who believe in him—so, when respecting his fans his own life reflects his appreciation of them.

"I'd better confess there are few parallels where Brown the Western hero and Brown the actor are concerned. It starts with the home. I don't live on rambling 200-acre rancho and I don't own a horse corral. I don't jingle-jangle down Hollywood Boulevard in silver spurs or drive around Beverly Hills in a 10 gallon hat (unless I'm on my way to the studio, that is). But in my way, I figure I'm still a pretty authentic Westerner. Our home is atop one of the highest of the Beverly Hills. There's plenty of the wide open spaces up

Johnny, reading fan mail in his library.

there – in fact it's is about as close to heaven as you can get on this earth. The view from our front veranda looks out at night over the city lights and always makes me think of a huge prospector's pan, overflowing with nuggets and diamonds.

"Maybe it's a little out of character, not living amidst the sand and cacti, but I'm figuring my fans will understand – for our home has deep roots, and for me, it's surely chocked full of all the things I love in life.

"First, there is Connie – my wife. We met where we were both attending the University of Alabama. Our love 'just growed' from there – and we were married soon after the Rose Bowl game that brought me to films. Connie is beautiful as all outdoors – a real pal, as well as a wife and mother – strong, faithful and loyal.

"Jane Harriet, our 19-year-old daughter, is our eldest. I say this humbly, and proudly: she is one the most beautiful young girls I've seen. We're proud too, of the fine talent she's evidenced as an artist. She sculpts and paints and last year won one of the top awards at my alma mater—which is hers—the University of Alabama.

"Second in our coterie is 14-year-old Lachlan, the son we prayed for. And of whom we're mighty proud. He is growing very tall, straight and strong – in character and in limb.

"Nine-year-old Cynthia is our auburn-haired beauty—Cynthia with the auburn brown eyes. She's going to be a danseuse (ballerina) when she grows up, she tells us, and her beauty and grace give promise to that announcement.

"Our youngest—and the real belle of out manse, is Sally—with jet-black eyes and the eager, flashing smile. Sally arrived in our home just eighteen months ago to accentuate the positive of our happiness.

"People have described our house as

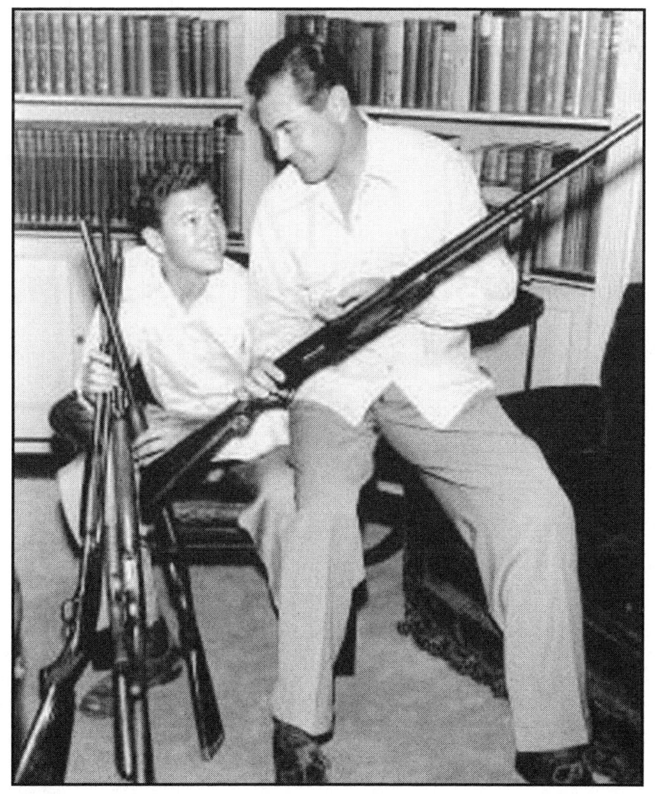

Johnny teaches his son Lachlan about gun safety (circa 1943).

'transplanted southern—furnished in 18th Century manner.' Well, have it their way. We do have an unusual décor. And we do go collecting very carefully. The wallpaper, for instance, in the entrance hall was made in France in 1825. Only twenty-five strips of this paper was ever made, and that which we have on our walls was removed from a French villa and preserved on canvas. In our upstairs hall is a framed serviette used by Washington. Delicately woven into it is a replica of the Declaration of Independence including the signatures. In one of the living room cabinets—and throughout the house—we have our accumulation of articles—some are museum-worthy. There's a silver pitcher—made by Paul Revere. We have the original bill of sale, too. And a paperweight with a coral top carved Cellini, and a singing shell which Douglas Fairbanks brought me from the South Seas while there on location for ROBINSON CRUSOE. We have model stagecoaches, too. We have a half a dozen or so, but our favorite we placed under glass. It is three feet long of a Plymouth-London Royal Mail. Only one-and-a-half feet high, it's complete to the four horses with reins. The coach has leather cushion, brocaded upholstery. and fringe on the top. There's even a coachman in the front seat, and of course, the fancy Royal Coats of Arms on the doors.

An early 1930s shot.

"The library is an all important part of 'our castle.' Its walls are lined to the ceiling with open book shelves and we've accumulated some 2,000 volumes – classics, novels, research, and adventure stories. I'm especially proud of *The Great Meadow*, autographed by George Arliss. And, although it sounds a little grim, we've an unusual book on Wild Bill Hickok which contains, in the cover, a strand of hair cut from Hickok's scalp by Leander Richards after Wild Bill's assassination at Deadwood."

GARBO, CRAWFORD, MAE WEST

(Johnny discusses Garbo, Crawford, Mae West and other famous actresses with whom he worked):

"Greta Garbo and Mae West give me the same reaction. When Garbo enters a room, or a scene, you know that *someone* is there. When Mae enters a room or a scene you also know that *someone* is there. When I see them personally, when I talk with them, when I play love scenes with them, I get the same reaction, the same sort of thrill.

"They are both supreme individuals—and supreme individualists. They are both egotists, 100 per cent. They both love themselves first and the rest of mankind afterwards. Their first interest is themselves. All others are subsidiary. In a sense, there are no others.

Johnny and the great Greta Garbo in THE SINGLE STANDARD (MGM, 1929).

"This is not so with other stars. Joan Crawford has her house, her little theatre, her various friendships and to each of these outside interests she gives freely of herself, her time, her heart. Ann Harding has her child, and her interest in the theatre. Miriam Hopkins has her adopted baby, her house in New York, and a variety of pursuits and occupations. Garbo has, primarily—Garbo. Mae has—Mae.

"They both have the most terrific warmth of any women on the screen today. When you are with them—you are acutely aware of them with every fiber of your mind and body. You don't take your eyes off them, because you can't take your eyes off them. They *matter.* They dominate the box office of the world today. They are *real*. Whether you happen to like them or not they are *so* real that every other person fades into insignificance beside them. They are *sex*. Garbo is the unattainable. Mae is the forever attainable. And because of this dissimi-

Johnny woos Joan Crawford in OUR DANCING DAUGHTERS (MGM, 1928).

larity they are *femme fatales* to all men.

"I have always been impressed with the similar power of their personalities. I remember working with Garbo in A WOMAN OF AFFAIRS. She came onto the set one day and there were some hundreds of extras in the scene. She spoke some lines – in Swedish. None of us understood one word of what she was saying. But the rendition, the sheer force of that great personality was so great, so stirring, that the entire troop of star-hardened extras, the electricians, props, and other players broke into tumultuous applause. Both of these women create audiences wherever they go. Every individual becomes a spectator.

"I saw much the same thing happen in this current picture of Mae's. We had a great number of prize-fighters on the set. Mae had a big scene to do. She did it – and not a muscle rippled on one of those burly, not easily impressed, fellows. You could have heard the well-known pin drop. When she was through there broke out again spontaneous applause. Those are the only two times I have ever seen such a thing happen on a set. They were not her fellow players, those fighters, they were her audience – and they were with her to a man.

Johnny is infatuated by sexy Mae West (BELLE OF THE NINETIES, Paramount, 1934).

"Their surface methods are different. Garbo is aloof. She doesn't mix with the other members of the cast nor fraternize with the men and women on the set. Mae does mix and mingle with everyone. She is the reverse of aloof. She takes infinite time and patience with the other members of the cast. She worked for hours with the fighters, coaching them, helping them with their lines, working right along with them. She didn't do what most stars would do—leave the set and say that she would return when they were ready to shoot.

"But despite the different methods, both get the same results – both inspire the same dog-like devotion, abject adoration. No one is ever *familiar* with either one of them. It is always 'Miss Garbo' to her fellow workers, and it is always 'Miss West.' If Garbo makes a serious, somber remark to someone it is received with respect and if Mae makes an amusing wisecrack it, too, is received with respect. Funny, but true. Both are indefatigable workers. Both have enormous powers of concentration."

Johnny recalled working with Mae West in BELLE OF THE NINETIES (Paramount, 1934), "I'll never forget a scene I did with Mae West: It was a love scene. I had to shower her with kisses. I told her afterwards, 'Miss West, kissing you is intoxicating.' She (jokingly) shoved me away and said, 'Well, I don't want to turn you into a drunk in only one night.'"

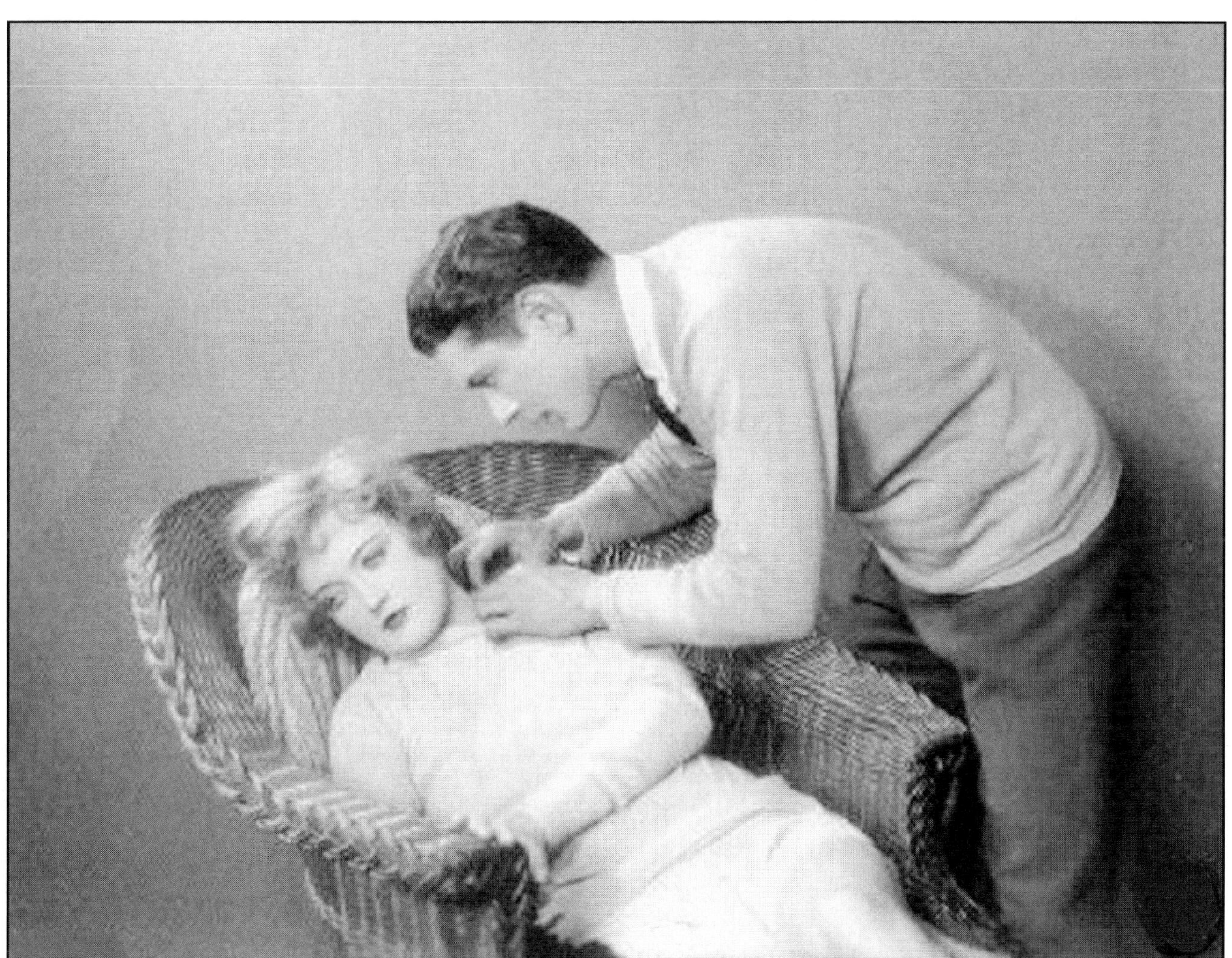

The Fair Co-Ed (MGM, 1927) with Marion Davies.

A TURN FOR THE WORSE

Johnny with "America's sweetheart," Mary Pickford in COQUESTTE (MGM, 1929).

In 1930, MGM announced that Joan Crawford would be starred in a picture called LAUGHING SINNERS. The movie was based on a Broadway play called "Torch Song." Johnny was also cast in the film (Bob Livingston had also tried out for the role). After previews of the film were shown, it was recalled by the studio and Johnny's part was cut from the picture. He was replaced by Clark Gable. Several have speculated as to why Johnny was removed from the picture: Bob Thomas, in *Joan Crawford* (Bantam Books, 1978), said MGM head Louis B. Mayer ordered a remake after a preview audience failed to respond to the original version.

John Douglas Eames wrote in *The MGM Story* (Crown Publisher, 1976) that production supervisor Irving Thalberg was prompted by "chilly audience reaction" to do a remake. "Thalberg detected dynamite in the Crawford/Gable combination and set the story department to work on scripts for it," Eames wrote. *In A Portrait of Joan* (Paperback Library, 1964), Miss Crawford and co-author Jane Kesner Ardmore attributed the decision to Mayer. Miss Crawford said: "Johnny's performance was excellent, but Mayer had seen the chemistry between Clark and me and thought he scented box-office dynamite."

Johnny, Madge Bellamy and Walter McGrail (THE PLAY GIRL, Fox Film, 1928).

James Robert Parish and Don E. Stanke, in *The Leading Ladies* (Arlington House, 1977), said Miss Crawford was displeased by the preview film, and they attributed the main responsibility for the remake to her. They wrote: "Her main objection was that the lack of chemistry between her and

Brown was making the product dull. She went to Mr. Mayer and put her arms around his thick neck ('He always responded to that, and he never touched my boobs or pinched my butt,' Crawford said). She asked that the picture be re-shot, but with Clark Gable instead of Brown. Mayer agreed"

Johnny Mack and Anita Louise in a publicity shot (circa 1931).

Eames writing in The *Motion Picture Herald* included some background in its review of the movie: "The religious angle has been soft-pedaled in MGM's picturization of 'Torch Song,' Kenyon Nicholson's stage play. Filmed under its original title, the feature was ordered back for retakes when, after its first preview, it was deemed too strong fare for screen audiences and likely to arouse unwelcome controversy.

"The audience received 'Laughing Sinners' as acceptable entertainment, though in the nature of preachment. Comment was made that the second title, 'Complete Surrender,' would have fitted the subject matter more aptly. The difficulty of casting the Salvation Army man is attested to by the fact that Gable was the second player chosen for the role. Johnny Mack Brown played it in the first version. Regardless of who should be given the credit or blame, the episode was the beginning of the end of Johnny Mack Brown's career as a leading man at a major studio."

Johnny and Norma Shearer in THE LADY TAKES A CHANCE (MGM, 1928).

(Author's Note: It could be that Miss Crawford wanted Gable for the part because, although both had spouses, it was well known that the couple was having an affair during this time).

Johnny's treatment by MGM bothered at least one writer. Carter Bruce, writing in *Modern Screen* said the following: "What about Johnny? When LAUGHING SINNERS was seen by studio executives they ordered the film re-made with Clark Gable in place of Johnny Mack Brown. Is Johnny through? Johnny is the type of chap who prefers a quiet home to the noise and acclamation of fame. But Hollywood took him and made him a movie star. And, now – is Hollywood going to discard him? It is the hope of those in Hollywood who love Johnny that he will take his sweet little wife and their darling baby and leave for home the day that MGM decides not take up his option. Johnny isn't for Hollywood . . . and Hollywood isn't for Johnny. He never had any desire for a dramatic career. He never had the self-confidence of a born actor. Johnny still drives the dilapidated little car that he had when he first came to Hollywood. Until very recently, he lived in a very small house, just as he would have done had he stayed in Alabama. He still loves to eat green onions and southern-fried chicken. He gets a huge kick out of knocking down those little clay pigeons in the shooting galleries at the beach. He continually brings home mutt dogs and keeping them as long as they will stay, just as he would have done in Alabama. He, unlike most persons in pictures today, loves to have the studio take publicity pictures of his wife and baby. His idea of an exciting evening is to go over to George Fawcett's house and have a quiet game of checkers with his old friend. Not exactly a wild Hollywoodite.

"There is not one characteristic in Johnny's entire make-up that stamps him as a part of Hollywood. Will there ever be another picture like COQUETTE for the boy who has a rich southern accent but little innate acting ability? Probably not.

Alabama is the place for Johnny ... the place where he can be normal and happy ...may he go there and find contentment. Here's luck to the boy who never should have come to Hollywood."

According to most reports Johnny's southern drawl caused some problems when sound arrived. It has often been told that MGM cut him loose from his contract, however, according to an article in one of the movie magazines, at the time, this was not the case. The publication stated: "Johnny Mack Brown has pulled a fast one on the moguls of Hollywood. Johnny learned that another studio was negotiating to buy up the remainder of his contract with MGM, so right away he asked for a release from Louis B. Mayer – and got it. And now he has an offer from another studio at several times the salary he was getting under his old contract. These Southern boys certainly have an eye for business – rumor to the contrary."

Johnny and Eleanor Broadman in a publicity still for THE GREAT MEADOW (MGM, 1931).

While at MGM, Brown received a lot of fan mail. One such letter was sent to *Screen Play* magazine in 1930: "Dear Editor, My favorite players are Janet Gaynor and John Mack Brown. I would be so happy if I just received one line from Mr. Brown. Every time I see him play, it makes me want to jump out of my seat and grab him. He's got something that excites me, thrills me and makes me love him. His hair and eyes are too wonderful for words. (Signed) L.T."

Johnny also had an embarrassing incident reported in another issue of the same magazine: "Johnny Mack Brown is taking the ribbing of his life for the non-practical joke he unwittingly pulled on his best friends the other night. Johnny had arranged an elaborate dinner party at his home for a dozen Masquers, with plans to take them to The American Legion to see the fights. Johnny, with his pals behind him, presented the tickets at the door, but not until the guests had filed into an empty hall did the doorman say, "Sorry, sir, but you came to see the fights that were held last night."

Johnny and Raymond Hatton sell war bonds in Texas.

JOHNNY RIDES THE RANGE

Brown went on to appear in films at Paramount, Warner Brothers, and Universal between 1932 and 1935; usually as a supporting actor in these films. However, it wasn't long until he started making the movies for which he is best known, and best loved – B-Westerns. It must have been a big let down for Johnny when he went from making pictures at the major studios, and with legendary film performers, to making B-Westerns and serials for small independent studios, but he made the best of the situation and seemed content. Serials were considered the lowest form of Hollywood filmmaking, but pride did not stop Johnny from agreeing to star in the 1933 serial, FIGHTING WITH KIT CARSON, for the lowly Mascot Pictures.

Mascot was founded by Nat Levine, solely for producing serials. Years earlier, Levine had aided in producing a serial that he sold to Universal. Sensing he could make a lot of money with cheap serials, he formed his own company and called it Mascot Pictures.

Johnny as Billy the Kid.

Longing for starring roles in films, in 1935, Brown along with Bob Steele had been signed to do a string of low-budget Westerns with the poverty-row studio Supreme Pictures. But fortunately for Brown and Steele, Republic Pictures formed by Herbert Yates after he took over Monogram (this is not the same Monogram that Johnny would be working for in the 1940s) and Mascot studios, both heavily in debt to Yates' Consolidated Film Laboratories film processing company, and made a deal with producer A. W. Hackel to release the Brown and Steele pictures under the Republic banner. The formal announcement of creation of Republic was announced on April 11, 1935

Although a poverty-row independent, Republic was in better financial shape than most small studios in the mid 1930s, and Brown's career began to flourish again.

Johnny as the Kid in BILLY THE KID (MGM, 1930).

However, he became so identified with Westerns that, beyond the mid 1930s, Johnny rarely appeared in a non-Western film.

Although Johnny was not fond of the Hackel films, some of them were considered his best Westerns including BETWEEN MEN (1935), BRANDED A COWARD (1935), THE CROOKED TRAIL (1936), VALLEY OF THE LAWLESS (1936), and THE GAMBLING TERROR (1937), Johnny said of the series,"Most of my Hackel pictures weren't that good. They were cheap pictures just thrown together. I don't know where he found his leading ladies. The first time anyone ever saw them was when I was supposed to do a scene with one of them. After the picture was over you never saw them again. I had been used to working with actresses like Joan Crawford and Mae West and Mary Pickford."

Johnny had played opposite Pickford in COQUETTE in 1928 and was required to talk like a Northerner. This did not set well with one critic, who wrote, "What have the motion pictures got against the South? In all the recent attempts to portray the Southland, particularly in COQUETTE and DIXIANA, they have failed miserably. These pictures have been the laughing stock of Southerners. It is unpardonable to hear an actor, such as Johnny Mack Brown, born and raised in the heart of the South, talking as though he were a Yankee trying to imitate Southern."

Miss Pickford and Johnny remained friends, and when Johnny's first child was born in 1929 *Screen Play Magazine* reported the following: "Mary Pickford does genuinely adore babies, even if she has none of her own. Johnny Mack Brown's first-born is just at present the subject of her particular interest. On the day of the christening, Mary called on the Brown family and bestowed a beautiful pearl on the child as a christening present. The card on the gift read, 'From Mary Pickford to Little Coquette Mack Brown.' Every year Mary plans to place a new pearl on the necklace. The little one is christened Jane Harriett."

Republic, after buying Mascot, would later use footage from Johnny's first serial, FIGHTING WITH KIT CARSON (Mascot, 1933), and in a couple of Gene Autry's films. Brown's next serial was for Universal and called THE RUSTLERS OF RED DOG (Universal, 1935).

He would make three more serials for Universal: WILD WEST DAYS (1937), FLAMING FRONTIERS (1938), and THE OREGON TRAIL (1939). He commented on making the last two serials simultaneously: "I'd do a scene for one, then get on my horse and ride

Joan Crawford with Johnny in MONTANA MOON (MGM, 1930).

over a hill and do a scene for the other. Back and forth I went every day until one or the other was finished. And I never once changed hats."

Author Alan Barbour wrote about Johnny's serials in *Saturday Afternoon at the Movies*: "The earlier serials were well photographed and inventively done. The later ones showed obvious signs of cheapness, including stock footage from the previous efforts."

In some of the serials he rode a white horse called Scout, a black horse named Wheezer, and sometimes an unknown horse. In his features he also rode different mounts until he finally settled on a palomino called Reno (lately Rebel). He was also seen riding Lucky, a pinto horse that was ridden by several cowboy stars including Jack Randall, George Houston, Dusty King, Raymond Hatton and Jimmy Wakely.

In between his cliffhangers, Brown worked at various small and large production outfits. Some of his other films from this period include BORN TO THE WEST (aka HELL TOWN - Paramount, 1937), with John Wayne, and WELLS FARGO (Paramount, 1937), with Joel McCrea.

After completing FLAMING FRONTIERS in 1938, and with no new screen jobs in the offering, Johnny hosted a weekly radio from New York show called "Under Western Skies." It consisted of short plays and Western music.

In 1937 Universal had signed Stanley Leland Weed (1910 – 1975) to a series of Westerns, and changed his name to Bob Baker. Universal had been founded in 1912. A few years later, the studio relocated and was called Universal City. Studio czar, Carl Laemmle, opened the lot to paying tourists to see how movies were made. Baker got off to a good start with COURAGE OF THE WEST (1937), but before long things started going downhill for the newcomer. It remains a mystery as exactly what happened. For one thing, he started off on the wrong foot when he refused to accept the studio's chosen screen name for him—Tex Baker—even though the studio had already printed up publicity ads for the series using that name. Some have suggested that Universal mishandled Baker's career. Others have claimed that after only a few movies, Baker became assertive as if he knew more about filmmaking than the studio. Frank Matheny (Baker's fan club president) wrote in *Western Revue*, "Many times Bob stepped on a lot of the boss's toes at Universal. And nine times out of ten he got his way." Maybe Baker got his way a few times at the beginning, but his stay in Hollywood was short-lived. It is well-known that most B-Western performers were not held in high regard by some of the studios, and that they had little or no input regarding their films.

Perhaps Baker stepped on his boss's toes one too many times. At any rate, he only made 12 starring pictures until the studio decided to make Johnny its top Western star. Baker would appear in Brown's first six features, but in a much lesser role than Johnny's. Baker claimed he was promised equal billing arrangements with Johnny. If indeed that promise was made, it did not materialize. It must be obvious to those who watch the

Leo Carrillo, Johnny, and Dorothy Burgess in LASCA OF THE RIO GRANDE (Universal, 1931).

Johnny and Ed Hearn in Johnny's first serial, FIGHTING WITH KIT CARSON (Mascot, 1933).

Brown/Baker films that Universal had lost interest in Baker. In one film, OKLAHOMA FRONTIER (1939), the studio even let Baker get killed. This should be proof enough that Universal was ready to let him go.

Baker is the only actor known to have made a negative comment about Brown: "Johnny thought he was better than I was. To my way of thinking, he's not. He did not like singing cowboys and he wouldn't let me ride my paint horse, Apache."

It may be that Baker's treatment by Universal extended over to Brown, causing Baker to only think Brown had an attitude of superiority. It is strange that, some years earlier, Baker told a different story when asked about working with Brown: "No personality clashes as we both did our acting and went on our own way when the day was over. I never fraternized with Johnny except while on the set and did not really get to know him."

During the four plus years he was at Universal, Johnny did three serials, 29 Western features—six with Bob Baker, sixteen as the lone hero, and a final seven with Tex Ritter as the co-star. In addition he and Dick Foran, another B-Western star, worked in the 1943 Universal Abbott & Costello movie, RIDE 'EM COWBOY. Bob Baker made a brief appearance in the picture as a bus driver.

After Baker departed, Universal brought in the tom-boyish Nell O'Day (1910-1989) to add some spice to the series. She would appear in 13 features with Brown. O'Day was a capable actress, and she was a skilled rider. She was often called on to display her skill on her favorite horse, Little Shorty. She spoke fondly of Brown and reminisced about the fun they had making the movies: "Johnny was a very skillful rider and an experienced actor, relaxed and easy, always knew his lines. A Southerner, he had easy courteous manners. He had a quick and keen sense of humor and was well-liked by all his co-workers, which is no surprise; he was a charming man.

Johnny in the 13-chapter serial WILD WEST DAYS (Universal, 1937).

"Johnny and I were swapping stories about our beginnings in films. Here is his: He had been made offers from every major studio in Hollywood. Johnny and his young wife put all the names of the studios into a hat, because they knew nothing about any of them. Luckily, they pulled out MGM, which, as you know was the most prestigious studio of all. So that is how Johnny Mack Brown first became an actor for MGM. Johnny was a splendid horseman, as we all know and eventually, over the years, became a very active member of the Polo Team in Hollywood that had many English actors as players. It is a fascinating, dangerous, and rough game, and two of Johnny's friends were killed on the polo field. This frightened his wife and she asked him if he would give up the game. Johnny said he loved the sport, but understood his wife's fear for him, and also the responsibility he had with his small children. So he willingly retired as a polo player and never played again, as much as he loved the game. He told me he never looked back and never regretted his decision.

"Johnny Mack was highly respected and admired by everyone who worked with him. He was a man who had great presence ... a many-faceted person, a man of accomplishment, friendly and easy with others from many different backgrounds.

Johnny in the Universal serial FLAMING FRONTIERS (1938).

"During the filming of one of our features, our regular doubles had been engaged by another company and we had to use two persons who had never before worked together. The man was smaller than Johnny, and the woman larger than I was. The scene being shot was a riding transfer involving me from my horse, Little Shorty, to Johnny's horse, Reno. The stunt was not going well for our doubles; something awkward happened with each shot. We were all taking a rest between scenes when Ray Taylor, the director, strolled over to the oak tree under which Johnny and I were sitting; 'Now look,' Ray said in his funny laconic way, 'you two can do this scene better than those people. Do you want to try it?' Johnny Mack and I both said 'yes' at almost the same time. So we worked out exactly what we were going to do. The cameras started rolling; we mounted our horses, got going to a nice gallop and then did the transfer. I must say it was neat. That was the beginning of many more stunts we did together.

"Johnny Mack was a fine person in every way. I never saw him after we finished the two series of films we made together, because I went back to New York and the theatre, and then off for several years to live in London and Rome. Once Johnny Mack said, 'You'll go back to the New York theatre one day and I know you'll love and enjoy it, but I think you'll always look back on these years of making Western films and you may have some good memories. I don't think you'll ever forget these films,' How right he was! It was a prophetic statement, bless his heart. It is true. I look back on those years with fond memories."

Nell O'Day went on to describe working with Fuzzy Knight: "Fuzzy was one of the most wonderful people anyone could ever have worked with. He was just as charming off screen as he was in all the film you've seen him play. All of those pieces of pantomime he

Bob Baker, Fuzzy Knight, and Johnny in RIDERS OF PASCO BASIN (Universal, 1939).

Bob Baker, Frances Robinson, Frank LaRue and Johnny in RIDERS OF PASCO BASIN (Universal, 1939).

worked out himself. He had a marvelous sense of timing, as you can see in his films. And he could talk to a horse and somehow you had the feeling the horse really understood him. Old Brownie was the horse Fuzzy rode in most of the pictures he made with Johnny and me. He was a wonderful person to get along with. I never saw anyone cross at him either. I don't know how they could have been."

After making STAGECOACH BUCKAROO in 1941, O'Day departed the series and Tex Ritter (1905-1974) was signed to team up with Brown. Ritter had recently moved over from Columbia where he had participated in eight features with Bill Elliott. Ritter and Brown's first film together was DEEP IN THE HEART OF TEXAS (1942). Universal had bought the rights to the popular song and decided to use it for the film title. It is puzzling as to why so much music would be supplied by those other than Ritter, who was an established recording artist and a former solo starring cowboy. And, it remains a mystery as to why the studio allowed Fuzzy Knight (1901-1976) to sing the title song on screen, instead of Ritter. Knight had been added to the series for comedy, for those who appreciated him – and many did not appreciate his comedy, or his singing.

Knight, like many of the Western sidekicks had a drinking problem. He went to a woman who had successfully "dried out" other alcoholics. When the treatments were over, the woman said, "I'll be seeing you." To which Knight replied, "You'll never see me again!" True to his word, he became a teetotaler.

Universal had also just signed Jennifer Holt (1920-1997) to a contract, and she would be the leading lady in all seven of the Brown/Ritter movies. Holt worked with several Western stars, but the films she made with Brown and Ritter remained her favorites. She said, "Johnny Mack Brown and Tex Ritter were the nicest men. When I am asked about my favorite cowboys, I tell them it was Johnny and Tex. I loved working with both. When Johnny would say "ma'am," it was like honey was dripping from his lips."

Fuzzy Knight, along with Ritter, and the Jimmy Wakely (1914-1983) Trio, provided the music – even Holt sang now and then. All in all, it was an enjoyable group of films and one, TENTING TONIGHT ON THE OLD CAMP GROUND (1943), produced the longest film title in B-Western history. Other long titles in the series were DEEP IN THE HEART OF TEXAS (1942), and LITTLE JOE, THE WRANGLER (1942). These titles must have driven the person in charge of changing theater marquee crazy. The last Brown/Ritter entry was the LONE STAR TRAIL (1943), and it was a good one.

Brown's Westerns for Universal were well-made pictures, far above the typical B-Westerns of that day. The musical scores and photography were excellent. The scripts

Publicity shot of Johnny with Tex Ritter (Universal, 1942).

Johnny with Nell O'Day in PONY POST (Universal, 1940).

were believable, and the running inserts added to the action. This and the direction by Ray Taylor, Ford Beebe, and Joseph H. Lewis combined to make one of the finest series of the period. And, Johnny looked his best, and he always turned in a commendable performance.

Author Mike Nevins, in his column in *Western Clippings*, wrote about the 1942 Brown film, THE SILVER BULLET: "By the summer of 1942 the producer of the Johnny Mack Brown series was Oliver Drake (1903-1991), who had scripted a number of the early Republic Westerns on which Joseph H. Lewis (often referred to as "Wagon Wheel Joe") had been supervising editor. Drake admired Joe's work and wanted to bring him back but, as he told me almost a half a century later, the front office said no. 'Every shot we have on the street he shoots through a wagon wheel. And we're so sick and tired of the wagon wheel shots. We don't want Joe Lewis.' Drake had a talk with Lewis and, after making him a promise to stop shooting through wagon wheels, got him a job directing THE SILVER BULLET. One day Drake visited the set and walked in on a saloon sequence. 'I walked in on the set and what do I see? He's got a wheel of fortune in the foreground and he's shooting through the wheel. I walked over and said: 'Joe you cannot print this scene—you forgot this wagon wheel—take it out of here. If you don't, I will. And don't shoot any more wheels, any kind of wheels. I don't care how big or small they are!'" But as anyone can see, who is lucky enough to have a print or cassette of THE SILVER BULLET, Lewis

Fuzzy Knight, Nell O'Day, and Johnny

eventually won the wheel war and was brought back to direct a third Brown picture, BOSS OF HANGTOWN MESA (1942)."

In 1943 Universal, tired of the Western format and its low-budget stigma, released Johnny. At the time, he thought his screen career was over, and that he would have to seek employment in another field, but fate took a hand.

Monogram Pictures, which had been re-formed in 1937 by Ray Johnson and Trem Carr, started the "Rough Riders" series in 1941 featuring old-timers, Buck Jones (1889 or 1891-1942), Tim McCoy (1891-1978) and Raymond Hatton (1887-1971).

In 1942, and after eight of the "Rough Rider" pictures, McCoy re-enlisted in the Army. Although he was now 50 years old, McCoy felt he could still offer something for his Country that was now involved in World War II. McCoy did not consider going back into the Army at his age such big deal and said, "I walked out of a contract at Monogram because the War was on. I used to say, at the time, that any guy who was physically fit to do the things we had to do in pictures ought to be in there doing his stuff. We had a war on – not playing cowboys and Indians. So I sent them a telegram and walked right off. They said they could have me deferred—deferred my eye!"

Then, after losing McCoy to the Army, Buck Jones along with some 500 others, died as a result of a fire at the famous Cocoanut Grove night club in Boston, Massachusetts.

Monogram, now desperately needing a Western star with name recognition, sent out a call for Johnny Mack Brown. So after only a brief absence from the screen, Johnny was back in the saddle again. In fact, he had been out of work such a brief time that some of the pictures he made for Universal were still showing in the movie houses when his first Monogram feature hit the screen. He went on to make more starring films for Monogram than he had at all the other previous studios combined.

His first film for Monogram was THE GHOST RIDER (1943). His character in most of these movies was Nevada Jack McKenzie. Raymond Hatton, a holdover from the "Rough Riders" series, became Johnny's sidekick. He was no stranger to Johnny since they had worked together in the short film HOLLYWOOD HALFBACKS (Universal, 1931), VANISHING FRONTIER (Paramount, 1932), and MAYLAY BY NIGHT (Mayfair, 1932). For a while, Hatton retained the same character name (Sandy Hopkins) that he had used in the "Rough Riders" films. He would later use various names throughout the series. Hatton had worked in some highly regarded movies, and was considered an outstanding actor during the silent era. He had also appeared as a sidekick to Roy Rogers as well as being a member in nine of the "Three Mesquiteer" series. Hatton was not the typical B-Western sidekick—he did not fall in water troughs, constantly suffer hunger pains, sing silly songs, or portray an ignoramus. Hatton was intelligent and serious, and he played a vital role in helping Johnny apprehend the outlaws.

One of Johnny's 1943 movies, THE TEXAS KID, featured a youthful, Marshall Reed (1917-1980). Reed, like most performers who worked with the amicable Brown, developed a great affection for him. Johnny must have liked Reed too because Reed worked in some 30 of Johnny's films.

Reed talked about working with Johnny: "He was the greatest. When one of his pictures was completed, Johnny would come around and thank everyone for working with him. I'll never forget the time we were doing one of his Westerns up at Walker's Canyon, near Newhall. I was one of the heavies and the good guys were behind us and they were shooting at us and we were shooting back at them. Now there were a couple of new boys on the job and we started the chase and were just about to go under the huge limb of a big oak tree when I heard a 'zing!' It turned out that it was the first time one of the new kids was ever involved in a picture and he had brought his own gun and ammunition. So he was shooting live ammunition. The minute I heard that sound, I knew it was something for real. Suddenly everybody scattered. Needless to say, somebody could have been killed. So they took that young man right off the picture and he was

Johnny and Raymond Hatton in their first film together, GHOST RIDERS (Monogram, 1943).

never heard of in the pictures again. "

In addition to becoming a fine rider and an outstanding Western star, Johnny also became proficient in twirling a pistol, and he did this in several films. A good example of his gun-handling can be seen in A LAWMAN IS BORN (Supreme, 1937), GHOST GUNS (Monogram, 1944), and LAW OF THE LAWLESS (Monogram, 1947).

Movie badman Pierce Lyden (1908-1998) commented about working with Johnny, and his gun-handling: "One of the fastest draws and best gun twirlers in Hollywood was Johnny Mack Brown. I played in shoot-em-ups with Johnny in the late 1940s and he worked with me on the fast draw and gun-twirling, but I never could clear leather or spin a gun like Johnny could; he was one of a kind. Johnny Mack was a good friend and I still miss him."

Johnny took on a different role for one film in 1945 when he appeared in one of his better Westerns, as a frontier doctor, in FLAME OF THE WEST. Years later, former B-Western cowboy star, Rex Allen (1920 – 1999), would make a TV series titled, "Frontier Doctor."

In 1946 Monogram, wanting to cash in on the singing cowboy craze, had Johnny sing in DRIFTING ALONG. The movie was not a good one, and his warbling was dubbed by Smith Ballew. Contrary to many writers' claim, it was not Ballew that dubbed John Wayne's singing some years earlier. When asked if he had dubbed for Wayne, Ballew responded, "No, I had never even been to Hollywood at that time."

After HIDDEN DANGER (1948), Hatton's contract expired and he decided to take things easy for awhile. He reminisced about the happy days he spent with Johnny: "Working with Johnny is among the happiest days of my life. No two people could have gotten along better; he was like son or a brother. I've had quite a career in pictures, and I made a number of important films during the silent days. When talkies came in I guess it was my lot to become a Western performer. It seems all my work has been forgotten except for the pictures I made with Johnny."

Beautiful, blonde Reno Browne, (1921-1991—real name Josephine Ruth Clark) made her first Western, UNDER ARIZONA SKIES (1946), with Johnny. She was a decent actress and, unlike many leading ladies, an excellent rider. The pair worked well together and she would go on to appear in six of Johnny's features, as well as in films with Whip Wilson and Jimmy Wakely. She and Dale Evans were the only B-Western actresses to have their own comic book.

Reno Browne spoke fondly of Johnny, "When I made the Johnny Mack Brown pictures, they changed my name to Reno Blair to avoid any confusion. They also changed Johnny's horse's name from Reno to Rebel. Without those changes, things would have really been confused. I found Johnny to be most gentlemanly. I loved it when he played the spoons. He used to get a couple of spoons and make rhythms against his leg. It was fun to sit around and listen to him."

Comic Max Terhune (1891-1973) was an addition to Johnny's cast in 1948. He worked in eight films in the series, starting with SHERIFF OF MEDICINE BOW in 1948, and ending with WESTERN RENEGADES in 1949. Terhune, along with his dummy, Elmer Sneezeweed, had been popular in the "Three Mesquiteers," and the "Ranger Busters" series. Terhune had been called Lullaby in the "Three Mesquiteers," and Alibi in the "Range Busters." He resumed using the name Alibi in the films with Brown.

In 1944 Jimmy Wakely had signed to do a series of Westerns at Monogram. One would think Wakely would be pleased to finally get his own starring series after some many singing and bit parts. At first, he was pleased but it was short-lived because he later said, "I had wanted to be a cowboy star when I came to Hollywood but about halfway through the series I decided it really wasn't for me. I don't care how good you are, you are not going to get anywhere at Monogram. Monogram was a place where stars were born, and where stars went out of the scene. So they would get beginners, and those who were over the hill to come there to make movies because they couldn't get jobs at the bigger studios. I came to Monogram to get going, and fellows like Johnny Mack Brown went there to die."

The disenchanted Wakely also claimed that producer, Scott Dunlap, favored Johnny over him, and took away his songs, and fancy clothes, thus ruining his career. If Wakely's statement about Johnny going to Monogram to die is true, it certainly took him a long time to do so. Johnny stayed with Monogram through 1952, when the studio pulled the plug on low-budget Westerns. Competition from television made the old B-Western format unprofitable. Also, by this time Monogram's president Steve Broidy wished to leave the poverty-row reputation of the studio behind, and Monogram's Westerns suffered the consequences.

In 1946, Broidy started releasing Monogram's better-funded B films under the Allied Artists name. His venture proved successful, and by 1953 use of the Monogram name was discontinued.

A 1948 issue of *Screen Play magazine* reported a funny incident about Johnny: "The most embarrassed parent of the month was Johnny Mack Brown. Backing out of his driveway, he sideswiped a corner of the house and put a rather large dent in the fender of the family automobile. That was irritating enough, but what gave Johnny the red face was the fact that his 15-year-old son, Lachlan, was sitting along side him in the front seat. Papa was just about to give sonny-boy his first driving lesson!"

Johnny's daughter, Cynthia, explained how Johnny's son, Lachlan, got his unusual name "What we are told is that Lachlan McGilvray (an ancestor on his Grandmother's side) was a Scot who came to America in his late teens and carved out a living trading with the Indians. He married a Chieftain's daughter, Sey Hoy Marchand, and had a son named Alexander. Lachlan raised his child to be educated and there is much history written about Alexander of the Creek Indians and how he tried to protest the treatment of the Indians to the King of England, the King of France, etc., and wrote to Benjamin Franklin and the like to intercede. Lachlan eventually went back to Scotland and it seems he may have had some of his one-half Indian grandchildren educated there."

In 1949 Johnny had supported Rod Cameron in the "A" feature, STAMPEDE (Allied-

Phyllis Coates and Johnny in Johnny's last starring film, CANYON AMBUSH (Monogram, 1952).

Artist). After a busy day on the set, Johnny hustled to his bank before closing time and was immediately confronted by a bank guard. *Screen Play Magazine* reported the incident: "Johnny Mack Brown became a rather red-faced customer when, he rushed into a Hollywood bank, he was stopped at the entrance by a uniformed guard and relieved of two guns. Johnny had driven to the bank from a nearby movie location where he'd been doing scenes for STAMPEDE, forgetting he still wore a holster with two six-shooters. 'I guess,' the bank manager later explained, 'the guard was taking no chances – and I can't exactly blame him. He just came to work a couple of days ago – and a gun is a gun to him regardless of who is carrying it.'"

Johnny's first starring picture in 1951 was COLORADO AMBUSH and featured badman, Myron Healey. In addition to acting in the film, Healey also wrote the screen play.

Near the end of Johnny's starring career, Jimmy Ellison (1910-1993) was added to his films to shore up the series. In the 1930s Ellison had played the youthful sidekick in the "Hopalong Cassidy" series, and in one of the Brown features, THE MAN FROM THE BLACK HILLS (1952), Ellison and Rand Brooks, another of the young sidekicks in the "Cassidy" series, were featured. Although Ellison was only six years younger than Johnny, he had maintained his slim and youthful appearance. Johnny had put on considerable weight by this time, and the scripts provided him were slow-moving and unentertaining. It was a shame for he had been popular since the early thirties, and was one of the more convincing of the cowboy stars.

Johnny foresaw the ending of the B-Westerns and said, "The cost of making the pictures is so high now that the low-budget films are in danger. The major Westerns will last forever, but mine may soon be forced into a sad ending."

Indeed, the era of the B-Western ended in the early 1950s.The films had become so expensive to make that the studios started taking even shorter cuts than the ones they had taken in the past. More and more stock footage was being used, and instead of a gang of outlaws terrorizing the towns, it was usually only three or four. And, the one-eyed monster—television—was keeping youngsters at home in droves and away from the movie houses.

Brown had proved to be one of the most popular Western heroes for many years, but with the death of B-Westerns, he semi-retired from the screen. However, he remained popular when many of his old films were sold into TV syndication packages in the 1950s, and Dell was inspired to produce a Johnny Mack Brown comic book series.

All in all, Johnny was pleased with his pictures, but not so pleased with the new breed of Western movies: "They stopped making my kind of pictures – the action Westerns; instead they decided to get into adult Westerns ... the kind where you can kiss something besides your horse. The pictures we made had a good plot and a lot of action. We had people tumbling over cliffs and swimming rivers. TV does the whole thing in a room and they film it in two days. They just let the characters talk. You've got New York actors in Western hats who don't know what a cow is – standing around talking." But he did have his favorite cowboy stars and said, "John Wayne would have to stand out in my mind as my favorite all-around Western star in films, and Dick Boone my favorite as 'Hec Ramsey' on TV. By my choice, I naturally don't mean to put down the rest of the old picture stars because all of them were great fellows and actors."

During, and after, his film career Brown remained an avid outdoorsman. He often went hunting and fishing with his good friend, Charles "Durango Kid" Starrett.

Starrett told of one unhappy experience while hunting with Johnny: "There was an incident where Johnny Mack Brown and I were almost killed. I received an invitation to join this fancy club. They invited me to a duck hunt and said I could bring a guest, so I called my good friend Johnny. Well, I had purchased a specially built Cadillac station wagon with extra roof reinforcement. It cost $10,000 – a lot of money in those days. As we started up the road on the way to the club, a bulldozer broke loose and headed right toward us. It landed on the roof of my station wagon. If it hadn't been for that extra strong roof, we'd have been killed. We did end up in the hospital with minor injuries. You know, I couldn't even sue the guy who owned the bulldozer! He was a big shot around there and my lawyer told me that if I tried to sue him, he would accuse us of being a couple of movie cowboys out on a drunken spree." Brown and Starrett first met while working together in THREE ON A HONEYMOON (Fox, 1934).

Johnny, Jean Parker, and Richard Arlen in Johnny's final screen role, APACHE UPRISING (Paramount, 1966).

Johnny came out of retirement in the mid-1960s for supporting roles in the films REQUIEM FOR A GUNFIGHER (Embassy, 1965 – Raymond Hatton was also in this film), THE BOUNTY KILLER (Embassy,1965), and APACHE UPRISING (Paramount,1966), which was his final film.

Johnny's fans were appalled to see him in these demeaning roles, particularly in APACHE UPRISING where he played a crooked sheriff who made sexual advances towards Corrine Calvet, and got pistol-whipped by Rory Calhoun. Brown commented on producer A. C. Lyles' hiring of him for the small part in the picture, "I'm grateful

Johnny's star on the Hollywood Walk of Fame.

to him because I know damn well that he didn't need me – and I can use the money, but how big can a role be for a fat old man like me?"

Jimmy Wakely also took a dim view of the former cowboy stars playing unbecoming bit parts, "A lot of our movie cowboys were offered parts after the cowboy movies went that-a-way, but too often, the roles offered were those of dirty old men or drunks—terrible parts. It must have been horrendous to take part in some of those movies, as some of our cowboys had been forced to do to stay in the business. I just hated to see the cowboys take on minor roles after their pictures ended. It really hurt me to see guys like Bob Steele and Johnny Mack Brown doing that. They were my heroes when I was still back in Oklahoma picking cotton. I worked with Johnny when he was a star. It diminishes the image that was in my mind of the star he once was. I think the image should stay there – the way it was. I didn't want to demean whatever anyone wanted to remember. I wouldn't want to be remembered by playing a lousy, low-life character."

Wakely was not one to hold back his thoughts. He had a reputation for being an egotistical, opinionated and a stubborn man. His attitude caused him to be unpopular in the music industry which, although deserving, is probably the reason he has not been elected to the Country Music Hall of Fame.

After Johnny's movie career had ended, he appeared in a couple of television shows: "Tales of Wells Fargo," and "Perry Mason." He also traveled for a short while with the Tommy Scott Medicine Show. Sunset Carson and Tim McCoy were other movie cowboys who toured with the show.

With his children grown, and with little income, he and Connie no longer had a need for their fine home, so they sold it and moved into a very nice apartment at the Park La Brea Towers in Los Angeles. He later took a job as greeter at a posh Los Angeles restaurant. The move to hire the genial and popular Brown proved a wise investment for the restaurant for many would come there to eat solely for the purpose of meeting the great Johnny Mack Brown.

Johnny and daughter Jane's grave marker.

Johnny discussed his retirement: "I have lots of time to spend with my family

Johnny and Connie at Christmas 1962.

and to watch the late show to see old friends like Lash LaRue, Dick Foran, and Charles Starrett, who was the 'Durango Kid.' I love to watch Westerns now as much as I did when I was making them. They've been so much a part of my life that I feel those pictures belong to me."

He also never lost his love for football and said, "Football is sort of like sex. You might over-emphasize it, but you will never make it unpopular."

In 1970, Johnny was featured in a large layout in *Esquire* magazine in an article discussing the great athletes of yesterday.

Johnny Mack Brown lived an exciting and fun-filled life. He had been a star athlete, worked with some of Hollywood's legendary performers, enjoyed a long and happy marriage, fathered four fine children, and become one of the best and longest lasting of all the cowboy stars. He was not boastful, but he was pleased with his life's accomplishments. He expressed no regrets and said, "Don't feel sorry for me after I'm gone. I've had a full life and I've done just about everything a man could want to do."

Johnny's brother, Harry, said of Johnny, "His movie success never changed Johnny; it did not affect him one bit. He was the same easy-going guy he had always been. He and his wife Connie got married in 1926. They never parted and had four fine kids. Johnny loved making those Westerns. He was always the outdoor type and enjoyed riding."

In his book, *Great Western Stars*, James Robert Parrish wrote of Johnny's passing: "*The Johnny Mack Brown who had maneuvered through so many exciting screen chases and saddle rides was no more, but his memory will linger as long as movie audiences enjoy Western films.*" This was a fitting tribute to a man who was a hero to millions of children that frequented the Saturday matinees in the bygone days of the beloved B-Western movies.

Johnny is one of the few cowboy stars to be honored with a star on Hollywood Boulevard Walk of Fame. The star is located at 6501 Hollywood Boulevard.

Johnny's marker is located in the Court of Freedom, Columbarium of Heavenly Peace section of Forest Lawn Cemetery in Glendale, California (he was cremated).

THEY WORKED WITH JOHNNY

Tommy Farrell: "I worked with Johnny and he was by far the fastest and best at handling a gun. On one picture we were doing, Johnny was to draw his gun, fan it on the gunbelt once, fan it again in his hand, and then thumb the third shot. The soundman, Dick Young, said, 'Johnny, we've got to do it again because I can't distinguish the three shots. It all sounds like *one* – slow it down.' That's how good Johnny was with a gun."

Max Terhune: "After the Range Busters I was in one Rocky Lane picture, and another with Monte Hale. Then I got a call from Monogram, in 1948, as Ray Hatton's contract was coming to an end, and they wanted another comic sidekick for Johnny Mack Brown. I signed up for eight and I believe Ray was in the first three before he quit. Johnny was fine to work with—a fine Southern gentleman and a wonderful horseman. I did a year with him and, in one, I did my medicine show spiel, which I did first in White Stallion in 1944."

Pierce Lyden: "He was very friendly; we worked together in about 20 pictures. I had a great time with Johnny. He was always a Southern gentleman and that was kind of unusual around motion pictures."

Jimmy Wakely: "When Hoppy was dropped by Paramount my singing group moved over to Universal where we backed up Johnny Mack Brown and Tex Ritter in their series. Tex had an old white horse called White Flash known to us cowboys as a hammerhead—a horse with no brains and hard to control. He might've looked good racing across the prairie but his stable manners were pretty bad. He had a tough mouth and once he was in a run he couldn't be stopped. In the running inserts, Johnny and Tex would come riding full tilt after the camera car but when the scene was through White Flash kept on running. It took two wranglers down the trail apiece to close in and stop him.

"They were doing one of these scenes one day and Johnny Bond and I were sitting in the car listening to the radio. We were called in for a crowd scene in the main street. As we walked across the street to the saloon, Brown and Ritter appeared on their horses. Well, Johnny's steed just brushed me so I knew I was in trouble. Tex and White Flash were somewhere near but I didn't turn around. I didn't want to be hit full in the face by a runaway horse. Sure enough old White Flash hit me square in the back and sent me 15 feet down the street. I slid along on my front and my shirt buttons and gun belt were ripped off. I was lucky I landed on a patch that had been spaded over to make a soft touchdown for a 'bulldog' earlier in the picture. Johnny helped me to my feet—Ritter was long gone. Tex finally got back and sat down with me and put his arm around me and said, 'Damn Jimmy, what can a man say after he just run over you with his hoss?'

"Neither Tex nor Johnny was happy at co-starring. Johnny had been paired with Bob Baker and Tex with Bill Elliott and neither wanted to repeat the experience. I believe Tex was promised equal billing with Johnny but it didn't happen. It was always obvious who No. 1 was. As the series went on I got bigger parts but then Johnny left Universal. Johnny Bond stayed on with Tex and Russell Hayden, forming his Red River Valley Boys. I went to Columbia and was given feature roles with Charles Starrett while Johnny went to Monogram.

"Strangely enough, about a year later I was signed by Monogram and I found myself in competition with Johnny. I sang a lot of songs in my first films—as many as nine!—And they helped keep down the violence. But when Scotty Dunlap became studio production manager he changed everything. He had a business interest in the Johnny Mack Brown series and didn't like it when my series out grossed Johnny's (I have not found evidence of this although Jimmy insisted he had seen Monogram's returns. The Motion Picture Almanac does not list Jimmy as a Top Ten Western Moneymaker during his starring years, while Johnny is placed every year). So Dunlap cut down my songs and cut out my fancy wardrobe and made me wear Levis and plain shirts."

Bob Baker: "I learned the saddle trade at the Gilmour Saddle Shop at Studio C at Universal while I was working on the Johnny Mack Brown pictures. I would go over there and hang around and say I wanted to learn how to make saddles. The Westerns with Johnny were my last starring roles at Universal. I didn't like the set up. My agent arranged it. At that time, he was not as popular as I was and yet they set me behind him." (According to the Motion Picture Almanac, Baker was number ten in the Top Ten Western Moneymakers while Johnny was not listed).

Raymond Hatton: "One of the best series I ever made in my life was The Rough Riders with Buck Jones and Colonel Tim McCoy....perfect boys. You knew what you were doing... they knew what they were doing. After the first eight, Buck was talked into going to Boston by Scotty Dunlap who had promised exhibitors he would turn up. You know what happened ... the nightclub caught fire. Buck was badly messed up and died a few days later. We had services for him. That leaves me with the Colonel.

There was going to be another Rough Riders series; we had the stories and everything. We went out to the studio to talk to Dunlap and the Colonel, and then the Colonel went back up to Wyoming. So we're ready to start the picture and we get a wire from the Colonel saying, 'Rough Riders I'm about to go back in the Army.' Now I'm the Lone Wolf....who can we get now? They decide to get Jack Holt ... so they talked to Jack. We're about to get started and Jack says 'I'm going into the Cavalry.' I said 'Wait a minute—an old pap like you—what you going into the Cavalry for?' Jack said 'I want to go in the

War—I want to do my part.' So anyway he's gone and Hatton's all alone again.

Then Dunlap said 'We'll get Johnny Mack Brown, he's a big good-looking guy and he can ride a horse, he'll be a good partner for you. What do you think?' I said 'All right, but tie the guy down this time—either hog tie him or sign him up.' Johnny and I were together for 5-6 years. They were good pictures, but I had some property up here in the Valley and I had turned 60 so I dropped out. I said if anyone wanted me they could call me and I'd decide if liked the sound of it."

Roy Barcroft: "One of the first things I did was a Johnny Mack Brown serial at Universal in 1938 (FLAMING FRONTIERS). Fortunately, I was a horseman and that's what they wanted...someone who could ride, read lines and fight. I wasn't too good at fights at first. The first fight I did was with Johnny Mack Brown. The director shouted 'Cut! What in the hell is this?' So I went out and learned the techniques of a movie fight."

Beth Marion: "I felt sad about Johnny Mack Brown later (she worked with Johnny in BETWEEN MEN). He was just a maitre d' at a restaurant, and I went in this one time while we were still living there in California, my present husband and I, and I don't know to this day why I wouldn't make myself known to Johnny. You know, I thought, well, maybe he would rather I didn't recognize him. I didn't know what to do. He didn't look very good, you know, but he showed us to the table. Wouldn't you have wondered what to do? That's why I didn't, but then I was always sorry I didn't."

Bill Hale: "I made my first picture with Johnny. Of course, I was just starting, so it was a walk-on part. We made several pictures together, and it was always fun working with him. I guess, like everyone else will tell you, Johnny was a good man, and always a gentleman. He was an easy-going man that everyone liked. Johnny was one of the best ever with gun tricks." (I learned while talking to Bill Hale that his brother's name is not Monte Hale, nor is Bill's surname Hale. He did not care to reveal the name.)

Lois Hall: "It is tough remembering little incidents when you're working with a complete gentleman, but there were no silly tricks, angry episodes, or stupid mistakes. I just remember how nice Johnny was—kind, thoughtful, rather reserved, and a joy to be around. It was wonderful working with him."

Myron Healey: "Johnny Mack Brown was a real gentleman at the time we worked together. I never heard him utter any kind of profanity, which is more than I can say for myself."

Joyce Compton (She worked with Johnny in VALLEY OF THE LAWLESS (Supreme 1936): "Johnny was a dear man; everyone on the set liked him."

Jane Adams: "Johnny had a wonderful smile and he loved life."

Evelyn Finley: "My favorite leading man was Johnny Mack Brown. I loved doing three films with him."

Louise Stanley: "Johnny was pleasant in every way."

Lois January: "Johnny Mack Brown was a true gentleman."

Terry Frost: "Johnny was a nice man. He was a southern gentleman and had a beautiful accent."

Tris Coffin: "Johnny was one of the nicest guys in the world. He liked everybody, and everybody liked him. Everyone enjoyed working with Johnny and Bill Elliott."

Bob Kortman and Johnny in the 1937 Universal serial WILD WEST DAYS.

FANS MEET JOHNNY

(Excerpt from *Behind the Scenes, Western Movies and Television Shows* by Steven Lodge)

It was 1951, I was all of eight-years-old when I stepped out of our 1946 Packard Clipper with my little brother, Bobby, at my side—both of us dressed in our spiffy cowboy outfits. It never occurred to me that I was putting my young boot-covered feet on what would become hallowed ground for us B-Western fans—the dust and tumbleweed covered soil of the Iverson Ranch.

My aunt worked in the Publicity Department for Monogram Pictures and had arranged for us to visit a shooting set. 'It's somewhere out near Chatsworth, way, way out there, past the boondocks,' she said, as we traveled through the San Fernando Valley, never to be seen again, and down Ventura Boulevard, with its quaint, small villages, broken up by peaceful countryside, where mighty skyscrapers stand today. Then, up Topanga Canyon Boulevard, not much of a parkway back then, just a two-lane country road lined with pastures and grazing livestock, chiseled into the foothills at the west end of the basin—at present, an unstoppable city of concrete. The directions my aunt had given us were rather vague. All she had said was that we were to turn off on the first dirt road we came to after Topanga Canyon Boulevard turned into the Santa Susanna Pass.

It was our very first time on that steep and narrow, winding route—though it would not be our last. After a few worrisome moments, we were there. No sign; no nothing. Just a deserted, sandy path, stitched almost evenly on both sides, with sparse, wind-whipped weeds and rusted barbed wire.

Once inside the ranch proper, and without any further directions from my aunt, we had absolutely no idea where we were supposed to go. We felt quite lucky to see an old pickup with a man working beside it. After telling him we were looking for the movie set, he asked, "Which one?" It seems that there was more than just one movie company shooting on Iverson land that morning. We were more specific, and within minutes we were traversing an area covered with unique and colorful rock formations—Iverson's Garden of the Gods. We wound around a few more blind curves, perfect settings for stagecoach holdups or a good ambush, and finally saw a configuration of vehicles parked behind some old wooden buildings. This, as it turned out, was the Lower Iverson Western Street. And it was there that my brother and I started on one of the most memorable days in our young lives.

A whistle blew from somewhere and loud voice yelled, "Quiet!" We stopped dead in our tracks; it stopped others, too. My Mom was just getting out of the car when a man, one of a few that was close by, shushed her with a finger to his lips. "We're shooting sound," he whispered. 'Everyone's got to be really quiet." So we waited, and waited. We could hear nothing. Another loud voice yelled, "Cut! that's a keeper." People began to move again. I grinned to my brother. We were actually on an honest to goodness B-Western movie set.

Television had done it: "ruined us forever," my Mom used to say. My brother and I had become grade-A, certified, B-Western aficionados in the one short year since our dad had brought home the parts and assembled that one-eyed monster in our living room—it was a 17-incher, quite large for a TV screen in those days. Other things were shown on television back then, but the B-Western seems to have been the easiest and the cheapest venue for those early pioneers of local television to run day in and day out. We watched them all. We knew every cowboy who ever rode off into the sunset, and every outlaw, crooked banker, sidekick, posse member, and every horse's name.

Before Bobby and I even got to the main street, we spotted a very familiar face coming out of a small trailer. The man was dressed like an outlaw and had on dark makeup. Later in life, I found out his name was Lee Roberts, who was a pretty well-known bad guy in those days. We approached Roberts with caution because he did look rather sinister. He broke into a grin when he saw us coming with our autograph books in hand. He signed them both without us even having to ask. My Mom was right there with our trusty Kodak Brownie camera, snapping our picture with Roberts before he was called away. We looked at what he'd written and saw that he had also signed the name of his character – Slade. So it was Slade that we knew him from that time on, when we would see him on television.

Rounding the corner onto Main Street, Bobby and I had to duck back as two horses, pulling a rickety buckboard, rumbled by. When the dust cleared, there were cowboys everywhere, some of them smoking, some playing cards, others twirling their guns and joking and waiting between scenes for the next filming to start. Bobby and I gawked, shaking our heads in disbelief that this really happening? So many well-known B-Western faces—Marshall Reed, I. Stanford Jolley, Bud Osborne, Lane Bradford, Pierce Lyden, Carl Matthews, and Herman Hack—and a couple of stuntmen, too—Whitey Hughes, and Danny Sands—men I would later work with as an adult. Mom snapped a few pictures of the group. Marshall Reed was the first one to notice us. He was dressed in a blue banker's suit, obviously the head bad guy—my brother and I could spot that easily. He introduced himself and the others. They all shook our hands and signed autographs.

One actor gave each of us a bullet from his gun belt, phony ones, of course, made of wood and painted to look like lead and brass. On the street behind them, there were men carrying big boards with aluminum foil on them that was used to reflect sunlight onto the actors. Others were in charge of the microphone boom and sound equipment, rolling it all into place for the next scene. And the camera crew, with one man carrying the camera, a large, black monster with a canvas covering—called the sound barney—to keep the camera noise from being heard on the soundtrack. Others were measuring distances, setting marks, focusing, and there was a buzz of activity with everyone moving in different directions, all at the same time.

We walked around, still observing, while side-stepping a grip carrying a huge reflector. "Hey, you kids," echoed a voice, "come on over here. Let me see those guns of yours." We turned around and there was an older cowboy sitting on a bench—another actor with a friendly face. He motioned for us to join him. We looked to our Mom for advice and she nodded with a smile. Bobby and I jumped up onto the boardwalk and were welcomed with open arms. The man, whom we later found out to be Frank Ellis, checked out our cap guns and told us they looked like mighty fine shooting irons. We got an autograph and Mom snapped a quick picture. There seemed to be a huddle, of sorts, in front of the camera, and about six men whom we couldn't identify right away. Then a modern-dressed cowboy led a sleek, palomino horse over to the group.

When the huddle finally broke up a man, dressed in an all brown outfit and wearing a white hat tilted back on his head, mounted the stallion. As he reined around, facing us, we saw who we had been waiting for days to see; it was Johnny Mack Brown—in the flesh! He saw us watching, tipped his hat and smiled. My brother giggled, "He saw us," he whispered anxiously. "He really saw us." Johnny Mack Brown was right there in front of us—not in black & white either—he was in color, real, and alive! I didn't need to pinch myself to know I wasn't dreaming. My mother took pictures as he sat on the palomino. A woman, his female co-star we suspected, was led up beside him on another horse. We didn't really know who she was that day because "The Adventures of Superman" TV show would not debut for another year or so. You guessed it—it was Noel Neill, the actress who would eventually play Lois Lane in "Superman."

Everyone became quiet as the camera started rolling again. Johnny Mack and Noel Neill exchanged a few words, wheeled their horses around, and the director yelled "Cut." That setup was broken and the crew began to prepare for another. We kept our eye on Johnny Mack as he dismounted. Nodding a temporary goodbye to Noel Neill, he began walking in our direction. "Oh, boy," said my brother, "now we'll get to see him close up." Bobby was right—really close up! Johnny Mack Brown, the world famous B-movie cowboy and revered athlete, walked straight down that Western street and stopped directly in front of us. There he stood, towering over us, as craned our necks upwards he seemed to be ten feet tall. "Howdy, boys," he said with his deep Alabama accent, "my name's Johnny Mack, what's yours?" "Uh, Steve," I said nervously, mechanically holding out my autograph book, "and this is my brother, Bobby." Johnny Mack took our books and, with a pencil my mother handed him, signed both books. He spotted Mom's camera and, taking us gently by the shoulders, turned us toward the lens saying, "Smile for your mama, boys." He tipped his hat to Mom just as someone yelled out that it was lunch time. Johnny excused himself and fell in with the rest of the crew as they all retreated around the corner of the barn.

Suddenly we were alone, and the street was deserted. The equipment was left unattended, and horses were all tied to the hitching posts. My Mom said since they were all eating lunch, perhaps we should be thinking about doing the same. She pointed across the street to a building with a sign that said "Restaurant.". "You guys want a hamburger?' she asked. Our mouths began to water as we thought of huge piles of French fries and cool malt. "You bet," we said in unison, and began running toward the cafe. We bolted through the door, fully expecting to see booths and a counter. We were stopped by a piece of fluttering canvas, painted to look like a wall. Behind it was nothing but rocks, open country, and the cast and crew eating at one long table. Most of them looked up at us, and we just stood there with our mouths agape.

When mother stepped through the door, and saw all eyes looking on us, she announced sheepishly, "We thought this was a restaurant, but I see it's only a false front." One of the young and handsome cowboys got up and walked over to us. Since he had a badge pinned to his shirt; we assumed he must be playing the sheriff. He knelt down and asked if we were hungry. We nodded, as our stomachs were grumbling by then, and he turned to the crew and said, "Is all right with you if these little buckaroos and their Mom join us?" Every one of them nodded, and motioning for us to come on over and join them. The handsome cowboy showed us the way to the caterer's truck where we were given trays and plates heaped with hot food, and then he led us to some folding chairs at the long table where we were seated.

My mother thanked the cowboy, while nudging us to do the same. He tipped his hat and Bobby and I tipped ours back. He smiled and left to join his friends. "That's Lucky," whispered a bearded old actor who was sitting across from us. He was directing his hushed comment to my brother and me. We looked at him quizzically. "Lucky," he said again. "You know, Hoppy's Lucky." Bobby and I exchanged glances. We both knew that Russell Hayden had played Lucky in the "Hopalong Cassidy" movies. All of a sudden it hit me, and I said to Bobby, "That is Lucky—the original Lucky. You know Bobby, it is Johnny Nelson, Hoppy's first partner." I was so excited, I wasn't making sense. "That was Johnny Nelson, the good looking cowboy with the sheriff's badge, who helped us get lunch is James Ellison who played Johnny Nelson in the early "Hoppy" movies."

We spent another few hours on the set, observing from the sidelines, watching Johnny Mack Brown and the other actors do more scenes, and we got more autographs. We never did get to see James Ellison again, but when we got home and developed the pictures we'd taken, there he was as big as life sitting beside actress Pamela Duncan. We did not know it at the time, but Mom had taken the picture earlier that day when she had gone back to the car to get something. Since they were both dressed in Western costumes, she decided to snap their picture.

The Monogram movie company was still shooting when we called it a day and drove off into the sunset. Bobby and I sat in the back seat comparing autographs. We were both preoccupied when my Mom slowed the car and said for us to look out real quick. As we pressed our noses to the glass, our eyes lit up – it was the Lone Ranger on Silver and Tonto on Scout. We waved, hoping we'd be seen, but through the swirling dust of our departure, we left them behind.

RAYMOND HATTON

(Contributed by Nick Williams)

Raymond Hatton had but one occupation during his lifetime, and he pursued that occupation with a singular dedication that is not easily understandable in today's 'retire at age 65' philosophy. For more than 70 years he was an actor, either on stage, screen, radio, or television. Over 50 of these years were spent in motion pictures. Not having seen records as to whose motion picture career was the most enduring, it is impossible to draw a comparison, but surely Hatton must rank near the top of the list. In October, 1918, *Photoplay* described him as "a great actor."

In 1919, another leading film publication called him "a great character actor and one of Hollywood's most studious actors." In a 1959 magazine article, producer Alex Gordon spoke of Hatton as being one of the most interesting and more capable character actors of that time. One can only speculate as to the amount of critical acclaim directed toward him in the interim.

If Raymond Hatton was such a capable actor, the question logically arises, why did he not win an Academy Award? It must be remembered that the category of Best Supporting Actor—and Hatton was truly one of the screen's best supporting actors—was not established until 1936, some time after his most productive years.

Since they were unable to rely on accents, or on speech at all for that matter, actors relied on gestures, make-up, and costuming to depict various characters in the early silent picture days. In those days Raymond Hatton, a master at makeup, could, with equal ease, be a teen-age pickpocket; an elderly, refined lawyer; a Mexican bandit, a Russian spy, or European nobleman. In fact, the November, 1916, issue of *Photoplay* broadly stated, "Raymond Hatton can depict every conceivable character."

How was he able to depict so well the diverse characters he was assigned? Not by how he thought a character would act, but by how he knew a character would act. For example, for his role of a narcotic addict in the 1916 film PUBLIC OPINION, Hatton spent several days in the psychopathic ward of a hospital observing and talking to addicts. In his 1916 film THE LOVE MASK he portrayed an old Mexican. To prepare for this role he traveled to Tijuana, where he observed a former Mexican grandee who earned his living posing for tourists.

For his role of "Gewhilliker Hays" in the 1916 filmization of Brett Harte's TENNESSEE PARDNER, he went to the locale Harte had written about. There he found old-timers who had known the real Gewhilliker Hays. Through talking to them, as well as studying Harte's story and related background material, Hatton developed his own characterization. These are but a very few examples of the thorough manner in which he prepared himself for each new role.

A rather interesting anecdote from these early days concerns Hatton and Sessue Hayakawa, then a star and later a character actor. Hatton was appearing as a Japanese villain in one of Hayakawa's starring films. Throughout the filming, Hayakawa, who was Japanese, spoke only his native tongue. Hatton never found out whether Hayakawa was paying tribute to his acting ability or assailing him for his lack thereof.

Always meticulous about the costuming of his characters, Hatton was never quite satisfied with the authenticity of the costumes supplied by the studio wardrobe departments. In instances of deficiencies, he provided his own costumes. He maintained an authentic collection of hats, boots, and walking canes.

A photo taken in 1919 shows him seated in front of his dressing room industriously polishing part of a large collection of boots and shoes. This collection ran from slippers and ankle-high work shoes to mule-eared cowboy boots and English riding boots. In his 1925 film, THE THUNDERING HERD, he wore, from his personal collection, a dilapidated 1885 hat which had gone through two Galveston floods, a forest fire, and several shoot-outs with Texas cattle rustlers.

Later, for his role of Rusty in the "Three Mesquiteers" series (1939-40), Hatton recreated the mode of dress of the fur trapper of the mid-1800. His buckskin costume looked like the real thing right down to its whangs (the short leather fringes) which served a dual purpose on the grease-impregnated suit: they functioned as a place for rainwater to drip off from and provided a ready supply of leather strands used for tying traps.

Another authentic touch added by him in his later Westerns was his use of wrist cuffs; however, at times he supplemented these with gloves. Many working cowboys preferred cuffs to gloves, because they figured skin was cheaper than leather. The cuffs were used to protect the wrists when holding a roped animal. According to Western film writers', Fenin and Everson, in *The*

Always meticulous about the costuming of his characters, Hatton was never quite satisfied with the authenticity of the costumes supplied by the studio wardrobe departments. In instances of deficiencies, he provided his own costumes.

Westerns from Silents to Cinerama, his cuffs were authenticated by their rope burns.

Hatton was born on July 7, 1892, in Red Oak, Iowa. It was there that he gained his first acting experience when he was about six. A traveling tent-show production of "Uncle Tom's Cabin" had arrived in town one day without a "Little Eva." Young Raymond secured the part and began his acting career by going to heaven by rope and pulley twice a day. His parents, Dr. John B. Hatton, a prominent physician and surgeon, and Anna M. Hatton, reluctantly permitted him to go on tour—consigned to the care of the production manager's wife. He remained with the show until a change of his voice sent him back home.

He returned to Des Moines, where his parents were living, to re-enter school. The call of the stage was too strong, however, and it wasn't long before he ran away from home to join another road show. This time he played in "The House That Jack Built." After the tour, he joined a St. Louis-based repertory company and toured as a boy comedian. The touring led to New York, where he found work in short comedy films at various studios. At one of these, Biograph, young Hatton met and worked with Mack Sennett. He was impressed with Sennett's abilities, and when Sennett left Biograph to form Keystone, Hatton went along. Accompanying them in the change was Mabel Normand, the beautiful and naturally-talented comedienne.

Hatton made numerous films for Keystone but ended his association when one of his films resulted in a near-tragedy. While playing an elderly Russian, costumed in a beard and long, flowing robe, the robe caught on fire and he was hospitalized and treated for burns. After leaving the hospital, he joined the Jesse L. Lasky Feature Play Company. His first film under the banner was THE CIRCUS MAN (1914). Co-authored by Cecil B. DeMille and George B. McCutcheon, the film featured Hatton as a hunchback. In another early effort, the 1915 version of THE GIRL OF THE GOLDEN WEST, he played Castro, a Mexican. The film, which starred Theodore Roberts and Mabel Van Buren, had as one of the most spectacular moments, his executing a breathtaking 200 foot fall down a mountain side. Filmmaking was certainly no sissy sport in those days.

To illustrate Hatton's versatility in his early screen career, attention should be called to some of his roles. IN THE UNAFRAID (1915) he appeared as a Russian valet, in THE WILD GOOSE CHASE (1915), as Ina Claire's henpecked father; in JOAN THE WOMAN (1917), as King Charles VIII of France. And in TEMPTATION (1916), THE LITTLE AMERICAN (1917), and WE CAN'T HAVE EVERYTHING (1918) as a variety of European noblemen. In KINDLING (1915) and THE GOLDEN CHANCE (1915) he played a crook; in THE WOMAN GOD FORGOT (1917) he was Montezuma; and in MALE AND FEMALE (1919) he was a foppish dandy. In this era, Hatton fulfilled a character actor's dream. He was given a starring role in Cecil B. DeMille's The WHISPERING CHORUS (1918). He considers it his best and, quite naturally, favorite role. Cast as John Trimble, he was supported by Kathlyn Williams, Edythe Chapman, Elliott Dexter, and Noah Beery.

Exhibitor's Trade Review, one of the leading trade magazines of the day, had this to say about Hatton in THE WHISPERING CHORUS, "Raymond Hatton as 'John Trimble' plays a dual role of embezzler and the outcast 'Martin' with power and discernment. His make-up is particularly ingenious, and one could scarcely imagine a greater contrast than he presents between the respectable husband of Jane, and the haggard broken man who is not recognized by his own mother until he reveals himself."

As mentioned previously, in the teen years, Hatton was considered to be one of the screen's most studious actors; for that reason, his opinions on numerous subjects were valued. Some of his public utterances make for interesting reading today. For example, commenting on the role of the actor, he said, "The actor takes his place among the world's constructionists and his art must be co-mingled with the physical labors that are tending toward this end. He must reflect truth in all his portrayals, for the world is sick of lies. He must be faithful to his trust and to the canons of his art. He must be true to himself and, as the great poet says, 'He cannot then be false to any man'."

Of the future of the motion picture industry at the close of World War I, Hatton said, "There is no doubt of the future of the histrionic art. It is as safe as the Rock of Gibraltar. The screen has established a position for itself that can never be assailed, and now in these momentous years ahead it is up to us, men and women of the motion pictures, to keep ourselves and our profession unspotted from the world supply to that same world entertainment that will edify even as it entertains; laughter that will ring clearly in the face of impending gloom; truth that will outshine the pretenses of base imitations; love that is exalted, purified—even as we all have been exalted by the fires through which, in some measure, we all have passed."

In his early films, Raymond Hatton displayed the well-developed sense of the comic element that he brought from the stage. This comic element had been successfully used in the 1915 films CHIMMIE FADDEN, and CHIMMIE FADDEN OUT WEST. In these he appeared as "Larry Fadden," Chimmie's brother, in support of Victor Moore, another brilliant comedian who played the title role. Even in the role of "Gringoire" the poet in the 1923 version of THE HUNCHBACK OF NOTRE DAME, Hatton interjected more comedy than had been noted in subsequent portrayals of the role.

Paramount, wishing to utilize his comedic ability, cast him with another gifted actor, Wallace Beery, in a series of military comedies in 1926-1927.

The advent of sound limited the range of characters that Hatton could play. His voice was not suitable for roles such as a Russian valet or a Japanese villain. However, this had no effect on demands for his services in motion pictures.

In the early 1930s he was cast in comedies, mysteries, drawing room dramas, and gangster films. His participation in such films continued throughout the decade.

In 1932 and 1933, Hatton was cast in a few Westerns, and, with that, the direction of his career began to shift. He appeared in supporting roles with Tim McCoy (CORNERED, Columbia, 1932), Tom Mix (TERROR TRAIL, Universal, 1933), and a newcomer to Westerns, Johnny Mack Brown (THE VANISHING FRONTIER, Paramount, 1932).

At this time, he developed the character that was to serve him well for the next 20 years. The character called such names as "Sandy," "Rusty," "Banty," and "Juniper" and can be described as a grizzled, cantankerous, querulous, garrulous, and, in spite of his foibles, likeable old-timer. It could be said that Hatton was rather too successful in developing this character, because it tended to keep him type-cast. Even today, when one thinks of him, this is the character that most often comes to mind. But, type-cast as he was, his characterization remained in demand; and in 1938, while working for Republic, he was cast in a series of four Westerns with still another Western newcomer, Roy Rogers.

When Hatton was needed for the "Three Mesquiteers" series, more successful at the time, he was transferred. The comic role of "Lullaby" of that series had been vacated by Max Terhune, and Hatton was given the role. The two other "Mesquiteer" stalwarts, John Wayne and Ray Corrigan, played together with Hatton in two films (1939-40) before both Wayne and Corrigan left the series. When the series was recast with Hatton, Bob Livingston, and Duncan Renaldo, Hatton introduced the character "Rusty."

(Author's Note: Merrill McCord in his excellent book, *Brothers of the West* wrote, "Because Livingston thought Renaldo and Hatton were his acting peers and because he personally liked them both, the series he made with them was his favorite "Mesquiteer" series." Earlier, Livingston had been promoted from the series by Republic for bigger budgeted films, but when John Wayne hit it big with STAGECOACH (1939, United Artists), Livingston, much to his disgust, was once again a "Mesquiteer." Author, McCord, quoted Livingston, "From then, I became very discontented ... I had no interest in the

Dennis Moore, Christine McIntyre, Raymond Hatton and Johnny in WEST OF THE RIO GRANDE (Monogram, 1944).

"Mesquiteers," and I told them so ... I was on automation. I'd just walk through the things. Raymond Hatton and Duncan Renaldo came into the picture, and they were so enthused, I said, 'Hell, if these guys are that enthused about it, I guess I'd better become enthused myself.'")

Johnny and Raymond Hatton, one of B-Western's best known duos, in THE LAW MEN (Monogram, 1944).

After nine "Mesquiteer" films, Hatton left Republic for Monogram in 1941. He was now cast in what some Western fans regard as the best trio series—the "Rough Riders." This series, which was really an imitation of Republic's "Three Mesquiteers" series, starred Hatton with two of the all-time film greats—Buck Jones and Tim McCoy. With well-written scripts and the talents of a popular cast, the series proved extremely successful but ended when Tim McCoy returned to active military duty, and at Buck Jones' death.

In 1943, Monogram re-united Hatton with former co-star Johnny Mack Brown. This popular Western duo made 45 films before Hatton left.

In 1950, Hatton was signed for a six picture series of low-budget Western films for Lippert. The B-Western pictures had not yet run its course and Lippert attempted to draw its share of the box-office by offering something unique—two heroes, James Ellison and Russell Hayden, and two sidekicks—Raymond Hatton and Fuzzy Knight. This was the last regular series of Westerns in which Hatton was to appear.

Hatton's last Western film was the all-star Alex Gordon production, REQUIEM FOR A GUNFIGHTER (Embassy, 1965). He used his same old-timer characterization except that this time it was tinged slightly with nervousness. This film united him with two former co-stars, Johnny Mack Brown and Tim McCoy.

Hatton's last film appearance was as an elderly hitchhiker in, IN COLD BLOOD (Columbia, 1967).

Mention should be made of Raymond Hatton's participation in still two other phases of entertainment. He played in several radio programs in the 1930s and 1940s. He also appeared in many television shows during the 1950s. These were, for the most part, Westerns.

An unaware film buff might say that Hatton finished the active portion of his film career in low-budget Westerns and leave it at that. On the face of it, this seems uncontestable, because the production costs of his Western films were much lower, on a comparative basis, than those of his earlier films. Having seen many of his Westerns, and

Raymond Hatton in his later years.

quite a few of his silent films, at no time in Westerns did Hatton relax his high standards.

Let me quote from *Picturegoer*, a now-defunct English film magazine which said of UNDER ARIZONA SKIES (Monogram,1946), "Raymond Hatton scores as the hardened old plainsman who pals with Johnny Mack Brown." This might seem little in the way of praise, but I invite you to read similar reviews of other Westerns of the era, wherein no mention at all is made of any of the actors' performances. I consider the comment of *Picturegoer* as high tribute, coming from a reviewer who probably neither appreciated Westerns nor considered them an art form.

It should be stressed that Raymond Hatton was, throughout his career, a dedicated professional. He always gave his best to each role, no matter if it were a starring one or cameo. Even in his conversation and letters, he referred to 'my profession' rather than to acting or to motion pictures. He was, as in 1919 he had said an actor should be, "faithful to his trust, and to the canons of his art."

On October 23, 1971, Raymond Hatton's body was discovered in his home in Palmdale, California. He had been dead for several days, apparently the victim of a heart attack. His wife, Frances Roberts, who was well-known for her roles in silent films, had died just a very short time before.

(Author's note: Some years after the Brown series, Hatton was on location working on a Gene Autry TV show. One night, he and some of the other actors partied too much. The excessive drinking had made Hatton ill, and when he journeyed to the outhouse he started throwing-up, only to see his teeth go sailing down through one of the holes. Since there were no volunteers to attempt to retrieve the teeth, and since Hatton looked terrible and could not speak well without them, Autry sent his plane to Hatton's home for his extra set of teeth. After Hatton's wife searched the home, to no avail, she was taken to the couple's other house where the teeth were located. The losing of Hatton's teeth caused considerable delay in the filming schedule for the TV show).

FUZZY KNIGHT

Comic sidekick Fuzzy Knight, a long time Universal comic, studied criminal law at the University of West Virginia, where he had formed his own band, and in which he sang and played the piano and drums. The nearest he ever came to practicing law in the courts was in his role as a deputy sheriff to Johnny Mack Brown in THE MAN FROM MONTANA (1940).

Born May 9, 1901, in Fairmont, West Virginia, John Forrest Knight gave up his ambition as a lawyer, in favor of show business. He made his debut in motion pictures just as sound was becoming the big new thing.

Knight was tabbed "Fuzzy," not because of his whiskers but, due to his rather unique singing voice.

(Author's Note: Singing cowboy, Fred Scott, told the following story: "Al St. John got the name 'Fuzzy' when he worked with me. The part was planned for Fuzzy Knight, but for some reason, he wasn't available. The script called for my sidekick to be called Fuzzy, and they just used that name for St. John).

Knight's first major acting role was in HELL'S HIGHWAY (1932), but it was his performance opposite sex-pot, Mae West, in SHE DONE HIM WRONG that helped established Knight as a comedian.

During the 1930s Fuzzy appeared in countless comedy roles for various major studios. Included among his Western work, in the early part of that decade, were films at Paramount such as SUNSET PASS (1933) and THE LAST ROUNDUP (1934), both based on Zane Grey works starring Randolph Scott and directed by Henry Hathaway. Fuzzy also played the role of "Tater" in Hathaway's superbly directed TRAIL OF THE LONESOME PINE (Paramount, 1936), starring Henry Fonda and Fred MacMurray.

Fuzzy began his major Western series work as a comic sidekick at Universal, beginning with a series with Bob Baker in 1937, and ending some 13 years later with the Russ Hayden/Jimmy Ellison series by Lippert Productions.

After Baker had been featured as the star in a dozen films, Universal paired him with Johnny Mack Brown, who did not have a series going at the time. Brown had recently completed filming the 15-chapter serial, THE OREGON TRAIL (in which Fuzzy also appeared).

Fuzzy also joined the Brown-Baker series, but after the sixth film of that series, RIDERS OF PASCO BASIN (1940), Baker and Universal parted company. Knight stayed on and little Nell O'Day was added (in addition to the female lead). In many of the Universals, Fuzzy was called upon to warble a tune. His singing, like his comedy was a matter of taste – some liked Knight, while others loathed him.

In 1942, Universal acquired the services of Tex Ritter and immediately matched him with Brown and Knight for a series of six films. Sometime in 1943, Brown departed Universal where he had made 27 films and went to work for Monogram where he was to turn out an even greater number of films. Tex later went to PRC where he was to make his last series of Westerns. Meanwhile, Fuzzy teamed up with Russ Hayden for a series of six films before Hayden went into the service. He then joined forces with the upcoming Rod Cameron in a Western series.

When this series ended, and Cameron had moved up to A-feature films, Universal brought in Kirby Grant to join Fuzzy for a series of films.

The last series work for Fuzzy was in 1950 when he appeared with two former Hopalong Cassidy sidekicks, Russell Hayden and Jimmy Ellison, in a series of six pictures made by Lippert Productions.

In 1952 and 1953 Fuzzy appeared with Wild Bill Elliott in a couple of Monogram releases, KANSAS TERRITORY and TOPEKA.

Fuzzy continued to appear in films throughout the 50s but, like many actors of that time, he joined television, where he appeared with former Western star Buster Crabbe from 1955 to 1957 in the series, "Captain Gallant."

Crabbe told how Knight got the part: "When we were looking for a fellow to play the sidekick, I said to Harry Saltzman, the producer, 'When you get out to California, look up Al "Fuzzy" St. John.' So when Harry got out to Hollywood, he called Fuzzy St. John in. Poor old Fuzzy went in loaded. That threw him out of the series, When I called Harry to check on things, I said, 'Well, Harry did you find somebody?' 'Yeah, Fuzzy Knight.'"

In 1965 Fuzzy appeared in one of his last films, THE BOUNTY KILLER (Embassy), where he was reunited with Johnny Mack Brown, and a bunch of other notables including Bob Steele, Crabbe, Bronco Billy Anderson, and Rod Cameron.

Fuzzy Knight, the West Virginia law student who never got around to practicing law, died at the Motion Picture Country Home in Hollywood on February 23, 1976. He was 71.

MAX TERHUNE

Multi-talented Max Terhune, like Johnny Mack Brown, Tex Ritter, Bill Elliott and some others, was one of the most beloved participants in B-Westerns. He was not only a ventriloquist, but a super whistler, magician, mimicker of several barnyard animals, and a skilled card dealer. Also, in his youth, he was an excellent baseball player. In the 1920s, he was employed at the Delco-Remy plant in Anderson, Indiana, where he was an outstanding pitcher on the company's baseball team. He later played minor league baseball.

Robert Max Terhune was born on February 12, 1891, in Amity, Indiana. The state was a hot bed for B-Western performers—Buck Jones, Allan "Rocky" Lane, Ken and Kermit Maynard, and Steve Clark hailed from the Hoosier State. Max's parents were Asa and Nancy Jane Terhune, and he was the last of five sons born to the couple.

Before he left his native state and embarked on a show business career, he married Maude Cassada in 1922. Daughter Doris Maxine arrived in 1923, son Robert Max Jr. was born in 1928, and son Donald Roltaire was born in 1930. Max's son, Robert, became a long-time Hollywood stuntman.

In the early thirties, Max traveled with several country music groups. His versatility as an entertainer proved very popular with the audiences.

Around 1932, he joined the National Barn Dance in Chicago, Illinois. The program broadcast over a station owned by Sears and Roebuck. The station's call letters were WLS, which stood for the "World's Largest Store." While working at the station, he became acquainted with Gene Autry, Smiley Burnette, and Bob Baker.

In 1936, Terhune went to Hollywood and joined Gene and Smiley for the film, RIDE RANGER RIDE. Autry had gone to Hollywood in 1934. Terhune's first entry in the Three Mesquiteers, where he gained his greatest popularity as "Lullaby Joslin," was in GHOST TOWN GOLD (1936), with Bob Livingston, and Ray "Crash" Corrigan. After the several "Mesquiteer" pictures, he moved over to Monogram (this time as "Alibi") to join Corrigan and John "Dusty" King in the "Range Busters" series.

(Author's Note: For further details on Terhune's career, please refer to the chapter, JOHNNY'S WESTERNS—A DIFFERENT PERSPECTIVE, by Richard B. Smith III.

There has been much speculation as to why Terhune left Republic and the

"Mesquiteer" series. Some have writers claim he left, at the encouragement of Corrigan, to join him in the "Range Busters." Republic records show that, for whatever reason, his contract option was not renewed. However, Terhune told biographer Nick Williams, he could have remained at Republic, and that his leaving was the biggest mistake in his professional life. Perhaps Terhune and Republic could not reach a salary agreement.

Fellow "Mesquiteer," Bob Livingston commented on Terhune and Corrigan: "He (Terhune) was a great guy. There's no question about that. He was just a lousy actor; that's all. They (Corrigan and Terhune) had no business in the pictures in the first place, but that's front office. All he (Terhune) could do was operate that dummy, and he didn't do that very well. (Regarding Terhune's attempt at keeping peace between Livingston and Corrigan). "In his farm-like ways, he tried to be a pacifier."

Livingston went on to express his dislike for Corrigan: "Whoever put him into pictures ought to have his head examined. Every time I would make a gesture, he would parrot the thing. I talked to him a couple of times (about his acting). The guy was no actor, and he never was. I knew it. I'm in a profession. I'm very proud of the fact that I can act a little bit. The things he'd do on the set! It was his childish efforts of trying to steal a scene. There were many tricks of the trade, and I knew them all. If anyone tried to upstage me, I'd crucify them."

(Author's Note: The quotes by Livingston came from the excellent book, *Brothers of the Saddle*, by Merrill McCord).

John "Dusty" King also shared his views on Terhune and Corrigan: "Max was a great guy, and one of the greatest shots I ever knew. And he was a great card player too. He never gambled, but he could deal 'doubles' like a professional." King was not as kind regarding the other "Range Buster," Corrigan: "I never liked the man and would rather not talk about him."

Gene Autry said: "Max was a very likable guy, and very talented. He loved to entertain. He could have a crowd around him in about five minutes and entertain them all afternoon."

(Terhune, explaining why "Mesquiteer" series was so successful): "I thought it was because it offered something for everybody. For the girls, it had a running gag of rivalry between Stony (Bob Livingston) and Tucson (Corrigan) in each story. It had plenty of action and fights, and the boys liked that. I believe the kids liked Elmer (his dummy) too. And the adults, I think liked the variety of plots and scenery—and the beautiful horses. A lot of credit goes to Yakima Canutt. He directed the action and the fights. Not only did he direct, but performed horse falls, wagon turnovers, climbing and water stunts."

Some writers credit Terhune with instructing Bob Baker with his acting, but Terhune said, "I never made a picture with Bob Baker. I worked with him on the National Barn Dance in Chicago. When he got an audition at Universal, he visited my home in Burbank and I gave some advice. I never took him "under my wing." He brought his audition script to my home, and I gave him some advice and helped him rehearse and how to read the lines, and he won the audition over seven others."

(Author's Note: One of the seven who auditioned was Roy Rogers.)

Max discussed his career: "I still don't understand entertainment. I was against radio because I thought it would ruin vaudeville. Then I was against the movies because I thought it was hurting radio. And I was against television because it was hurting Hollywood. I ended up in all of them. I loved every minute of it and have wonderful memories. I have had the opportunity of working with some of the most talented people on earth."

Loveable, Max Terhune, died on June 5, 1973, at Cottonwood, Arizona. He is buried in Clarksville, Arizona.

Kay Morley, Myron Healy, Johnny, and Max Terhune with his dummy, Elmer Sneezeweed, in TRAIL'S END (Monogram, 1949).

JOHNNY'S WESTERNS – A DIFFERENT PERSPECTIVE

by Richard B. Smith, III

(Author's Note: While I have covered Johnny's Western career, I thought the readers might like a different perspective on his cowboy films. I am indebted to author/historian, Richard B. Smith III, for his contribution).

Signing with Metro-Goldwyn-Mayer shortly upon reaching Hollywood in 1927, Johnny Mack Brown was initially assigned to drawing-room roles of a dramatic nature opposite more notable actresses such as Greta Garbo and Joan Crawford for the next three years.

Johnny probably pacted an MGM term-pictures contract, which availed him the opportunity for thesping with more Hollywood motion picture studios such as Fox Film, United Artists, RKO Radio, Columbia, and Pathe.

The Alabama native, upon doing MONTANA MOON (1930), his first MGM A-Western was backed up next with an even bigger budget for the studio's BILLY THE KID (1930). It featured him portraying the infamous 19th Century outlaw on MGM's Realife, a big-screen process.

But for Brown, the screenplay turned out as a whitewashed version of killer William Bonney directed by King Vidor. Former silent western, William S. Hart, visited the BILLY THE KID set, and presented a happy Brown one of Bonney's original guns with Vidor looking on.

Following work on THE GREAT MEADOW (1931), another oater, and a Clark Gable feature titled THE SECRET SIX (l931), Brown, learning his contract would not be renewed, left MGM.

Johnny Mack snared his next outdoor Western with Universal Pictures being LASCA OF THE RIO GRANDE (1931), then journeyed to Paramount Studios for a lead in the minor adventure VANISHING FRONTIER (1932).

Still mixing regular B-dramas with oaters through 1934, Brown got his first taste of how much stamina he'd need a year earlier doing a Nat Levine-produced 12-chapter serial for Mascot Pictures. The cliffhanger, FIGHTING WITH KIT CARSON (1933), was probably done on an approximate $65,000 budget with camera shooting sometime in May, 1933. The script focused on a gang chief and his Mystery Riders after stolen gold.

More cliffhanger work came for the Alabaman as he rode the range in THE RUSTLERS OF RED DOG (1935) that was produced around October, 1934. This 12-chapter Universal serial found Johnny having pals Raymond Hatton and Walter Miller help him protect a wagon train from marauding Indians and assorted outlaws.

Johnny Mack eventually drifted into B-Westerns by early summer 1935 because of a contractual arrangement he made with independent producer A. W. Hackel's very low budgeted Supreme Pictures. Such outdoor fare would be natural for Brown as he was an excellent horseman. Johnny did eight B-Westerns for Hackel in the 1935-1936 film season that involved him in pursuit of family killers, stagecoach thieves, phantom murderers, cattle rustlers, and crooked gambling. Leading ladies who were the cowgirls with Johnny in such movies as BRANDED A COWARD (1935), BETWEEN MEN (1935), VALLEY OF THE LAWLESS (1936), and THE CROOKED TRAIL (1936) where he severely pummeled player John Merton, consisted of Billie Seward, Beth Marion, Helen Erickson, Joyce Compton, Sheila Mannors, and Lois January.

Despite their low costs (probably $10,000 on average), each was hailed by critics as excellent storylines no doubt enhanced by Brown's tough fisticuffing.

Hackel, possibly strained for finances to continue his Supreme output, signatured a 59-page agreement on June 15, 1936, with Republic Productions. Supreme was still the producing company. Johnny Mack came on board once the new pact was a done deal. Joining him in this continued venture was fellow Supreme saddle star Bob Steele. Negative costs were to average $13,000 each. All sound-stage needs for the inside shots would be finished at International Studio, on Sunset Boulevard, in Hollywood.

Johnny Mack's initial B-hayburner under the new Republic arrangement was UNDERCOVER MAN (1936) that rolled before camera July 23, 1936, at Walker Ranch, a familiar site he was to visit many times in future years for film production. In this feature, he played an undercover Wells Fargo agent on the trail of horse thieves.

These later Hackel oaters featured Johnny Mack going up against more stock rustlers, crooked gambling, a range war, scheming ranch hands, land grabbers, in addition to fighting between squatters and rangers. Standout movies in the last of eight Brown mainlined were TRAIL OF VENGENANCE (1937) and GUNS IN THE DARK (1937). His female leads were Suzanne Kaaren, Iris Meredith, Louise Stanley, and Claire Rochelle.

As the 1936-1937 filming program with Hackel was ending, Johnny Mack temporarily left after GUNS IN THE DARK finished lensing in mid-February 1937, to take a Universal commitment on WILD WEST DAYS (1937), the studio's 13-chapter serial about three frontier cowboys who come to the aid of a beleaguered brother and sister fighting off siege of their ranch by outlaws after gold on the property. WILD WEST DAYS, an expanded version of Universal's earlier LAW AND ORDER (1932) screenplay, ended filming March 30, 1937.

It was back to Hackel for Brown who wound his eighth and end B-Western with the producer on BOOT HILL BRIGADE (1937) May 8, 1937. Johnny Mack decided not to renew for more Hackel products as he deemed such movie fare too cheaply made.

Johnny in a Confederate uniform from the Joel McCrea starring movie WELLS FARGO (Paramount, 1937).

Following two months of non-acting, Brown made his way to Paramount Pictures where he returned to the saddle groove for WELLS FARGO (1937), the big movie company's $1.5 million A-Western epic which shot footage July 15, 1937-September 25, 1937, and starred Joel McCrea. In this outdoor tale, Johnny Mack was a Confederate officer, Talbot Carter, who met an early demise. By August 20, 1937, Brown was doing another Paramount stint in a B-type trail-herd oater, BORN TO THE WEST (1937), where he lost leading lady Marsha Hunt to star John Wayne. It finished shooting September 4, 1937.

Gorgeous photo of Johnny from HELLTOWN aka BORN TO THE WEST (Paramount, 1937).

Brown, unable to obtain a new studio sagebrush series of B-Westerns, was beckoned again to Universal around February 1938 for the lead role with FLAMING FRONTIERS (1938), another horse-opera cliffhanger in 15 chapters, whereby he takes the part of an Indian scout who prevents a young woman's gold mine from being seized.

The man from Alabama then was off camera for a whole year until Universal summoned him for what would be Brown's fifth and final cliffhanger, this time THE OREGON TRAIL (1939), produced about February 1939. Here, Johnny Mack is a government scout hired to terminate Indian attacks on a wagon train for the 15 chapters.

Brown's B-Western rebirth became a reality by mid-year 1939 thanks to Universal. The semi-major studio had produced hard-riding gallopers for over two decades going back to silent days with some of

Hollywood's best movie cowboys who included Harry Carey, Sr., Ken Maynard, Hoot Gibson, and Buck Jones. But Universal, interested in having no more than a single B-oats star at any one time on its lot, had signed the latest lead, Bob Baker, by August 1937, for a new Western series under auspices of producer Trem Carr.

After Baker acted in THE PHANTOM STAGE (1939), the 12th of his starring B-Western, Carr opted to retire and not renew with Universal for additional cowboy movies. The studio showed no interest in pairing Baker with another producer.

Then, in March, 1939, Johnny Mack contracted a deal with Universal to star in seven B-Westerns for producer/director Albert Ray Brown, now firmly settled in with a far bigger motion-picture studio than his Supreme/Republic days, was trio-teamed alongside Bob Baker, reprieved after his own series went into limbo six months before, and Universal comic workhorse Fuzzy Knight, movie acting since the early 1930s.

Despite Knight's success in landing many movie roles prior to joining Brown, Fuzzy's acting ability was mediocre because he hammed it up as if constantly gasping for breath or had a mouth full of mush.

With budgets averaging $75,000 each (my estimate), Brown officially returned to the B-stable at Universal with the initial outing of DESPERATE TRAILS (1939), produced May 31, 1939 – June 12, 1939. Each of Johnny Mack's movies would have about a two-

Johnny, Frances Robinson, Clarence Wilson and Russell Simpson in DESPERATE TRAILS (Universal, 1939).

week shooting time frame.

Brown's character portrayals were of different named individuals who would be stalwart upholders of law and order rallying the outraged citizenry against rustlers, land grabbers, gold-strike thieves, crooked politicians, stagecoach robbers, etc.

Bob Baker was dropped from the Brown movies after he did six of them, due to reported work differences with Johnny Mack, once BADMAN FROM RED BUTTE (1940) finished lens work in mid-April, 1940. Baker set out to re-establish himself again as a B-Western star, but didn't achieve success. Bob came close, however, once! Republic Pictures' "The Three Mesquiteers" Western series had the studio in July 1940, looking at stars for its new sagebrush trio. Baker was selected as Tucson Smith, but then replaced at the last minute by more seasoned B-actioner Bob Steele.

Now that Baker had departed Universal, Brown and Knight rested two months from studio cameras until the 1940-1941 production season began June 21, 1940, with dramatics for SON OF ROARING DAN (1940). Instead of a different leading lady as he had for his initial Universal B-Westerns such as Anne Gwynne, Frances Robinson, Peggy Moran, and Doris Weston, Johnny Mack Brown was to welcome aboard, on SON OF ROARING DAN, an excellent female-riding actress in the form of Nell O'Day.

O'Day and Brown were to double the horse-action segments for movie-theater audiences at the Saturday matinee. O'Day committed herself to 13 Brown hayburners ending on FIGHTING BILL FARGO (1941), which finished lensing about September 5, 1941, well into the 1941-1942 camera period for Johnny Mack and Fuzzy Knight.

Just after Brown ended shots for ARIZONA CYCLONE (1941) in late June 1941, he landed a good Universal lead role with the Bud Abbott/Lou Costello A-Western comedy RIDE 'EM COWBOY (1942), which filmed June 30, 1941 – August 10, 1941. Brown portrayed ranch foreman Alabama Brewster who contended with Bud and Lou's usual screen antics – this time set in the Old West.

Once Johnny Mack completed FIGHTING BILL FARGO, Universal was evidently considering a sharp reduction for the studio's B-Western output as Brown was off camera for almost eight months until THE SILVER BULLET (1942) commenced camera needs May 1, 1942.

Universal then stepped up doing Brown's B-Westerns. The studio decided with advent of filming his TENTING TONIGHT ON THE OLD CAMP GROUND (1942) on June 22, 1942, to bring in veteran B-action cowboy singer Tex Ritter to equally compliment Johnny Mack with seven stronger screenplays which finished in very quick succession with THE LONE STAR TRAIL (1943) that ended shooting around September 25, 1942. Relatively new actress Jennifer Holt was the leading lady for every entry.

In the meantime, Tex Ritter was riding a strong B-Western wave having done oaters starting in 1936 for Grand National that amounted to 12 by end of June 1938, 20 at Monogram Pictures through mid-April 1941, and finally, Columbia Pictures co-starring with Wild Bill Elliott on eight fast paced hayburners that ended on April 15, 1942.

Johnny and Bob Baker in WEST OF CARSON CITY (Universal, 1940).

After the LONE STAR TRAIL wound up shooting, Ritter was to remain just through the end of 1943 at Universal for only production of three more studio-budgeted horse operas. But for Brown, a roll of the dice came up snake eyes.

Universal evidently decided against renewing Johnny Mack's contract beyond the 28 he'd done, because the studio was heavily trending more and more to A-film products that included bigger-costing Westerns. That meant exiting distribution of B-movies as quickly as possible. And, also, Brown was receiving likely a bigger salary increase each year.

Universal was to lense only 18 addition B-Westerns through end of July 1946, before halting their production permanently. Besides the three Ritter's, one would be headed by ex-Columbia and Paramount B-saddler Russell Hayden, six with action lead Rod Cameron, and one starring feature player Eddie Dew, and a final seven headed by cowboy singer Kirby Grant, who wrapped it all up with GUNMAN'S CODE (1946). All 18 would continue Fuzzy Knight as the perennial Universal sidekick comic.

No longer officially with Universal, Johnny Mack Brown found himself without movie work. In the meantime, low-budget Monogram Pictures, a prolific B-Western distributor going back to 1931, had just finished its first film season of "The Rough Riders" series of eight action horse operas in 30 days, portraying respectively U S. marshals—Buck Roberts, Tim McCall, and Sandy Hopkins, prior to Brown ending it at Universal on THE LONE

STAR TRAIL. The series under producer Scott Dunlap's guidance and mainlined by Western greats Buck Jones, Tim McCoy, and Raymond Hatton. These budgeters, at $80,000 apiece with inflated overheads, were going great guns during showings at small town U. S. movie theaters.

However, there came a series disruption following WEST OF THE LAW (1942) going in the can at conclusion of August 1942. This occurrence happened because McCoy, U. S. Army Reserves Colonel, entered World War II military duty despite his 51 years of age.

Monogram, rebounding on McCoy's loss from "The Rough Riders," went into a second season of features with Jones, Hatton, and seasoned movie westerner Rex Bell two months later by placing DAWN ON THE GREAT DIVIDE (1942) before lenses about October 8, 1942. The latest Jones effort ran almost 10 minutes longer, and possibly received an upped budget in the $90,000 range.

Then tragedy struck! Buck Jones, while on a war-bond tour in Boston, MA, visited the city's Cocoanut Grove nightclub the evening of November 28, 1942. Jones suddenly became one of 492 victims severely charred by that structure's blazing inferno. Buck died two days later at the Massachusetts General Hospital of second-and third-degree burns.

Monogram, with Jones' sudden death, was thrown into upheaval as to what should transpire for its future low-budget Western schedule even though "The Range Busters" series, at $15,000-$20,000 per feature, was churning out films with stars John "Dusty" King, David "Davy" Sharpe, and Max "Alibi" Terhune. Tom Keene, however, had ended his Monogram movies by mid-March 1942.

While "The Rough Riders" series' long-range continuance was in doubt, Monogram studio executives apparently decided by early 1943 to revive these features, but without the same series' name. Old timer, ex-Columbia B-drama ace, Jack Holt, successfully completed Monogram negotiations to star in the new B-Western with Hatton, but the day he was to signature such a contractual arrangement, Holt received military duty orders.

Instead, Monogram rescued Johnny Mack Brown from five-months picture unemployment status by casting him as U. S. Marshal Nevada Jack McKenzie in the new B-oaters with Raymond Hatton continuing on as pal, Sandy Hopkins. There was no third partner for the "Nevada Jack McKenzie" series except an occasional male maverick in need of proving manhood or clearing himself of an accused crime.

Johnny Mack officially came back to the movie saddle at Monogram as McKenzie, astride golden horse Rebel on February 15, 1943, once cameras rolled for THE GHOST RIDER (1943), a story of McKenzie's search for his family's killers.

Budgets for these new Browns were probably still in the same $80,000 range. Productions schedule would average no more than six actual shooting days. With seasoned vet Raymond Hatton, Brown corralled a sure-fire sidekick winner in Hatton, himself a movie workaholic and the consummatedly wonderful acting professional who made over 230 features through 1942. Hatton had started in movies during the early 1910s.

These fresh Monogram screenplays would engage Johnny Mack and Raymond against the same criminal types Brown had faced at Supreme/Republic and Universal – especially cattle rustlers.

This law-and-order duo, almost every several outings or so, would have to stamp out such thieves, although the four-legged critters were never seen anytime on screen, no doubt due to prohibition of renting/hauling cattle on routine location treks at Monogram, Jauregui, and Walker Ranches.

Such storylines by Monogram writers contained taut action sequences, mystery angles, strong music scoring, and great fisticuffing from Johnny Mack, land grabbers and stagecoach thieves were other nuisances the scripts provided.

Leading ladies in these features for Brown, who was content to leave their romances to other young male actors, would be Beverly Boyd, Inna Gest, Ellen Hall, Shirley Patterson, Christine McIntyre, Jan Wiley, Nan Holliday, Lynne Carver, Evelyn Finley, Jennifer Holt, Beatrice Gray, Rosa Del Rosario, and Linda Johnson [Melinda Leighton].

It was sometime after production of the fourth B-Western, OUTLAWS OF STAMPEDE PASS (1943), lensed from June 14, 1943-late June 1943, or THE TEXAS KID

Johnny, Christine McIntyre, and Dennis Moore (1944).

(1943), done by early August 1943, that Johnny Mack went back to Universal. The occasion for such a return was to emote a bit with comedians Ole Olsen and Chic Johnson in their CRAZY HOUSE (1943), produced June 14, 1943, through August 15, 1943. The Universal theme, actually involving the studio, had Olsen/Johnson renege acting in a planned second movie.

Before or after Johnny Mack's 12th Monogram galloper with LAW OF THE VALLEY (1944) that wound about June 10, 1944, Hatton sauntered to RKO Radio Pictures for one day's scenes to portray the old, bearded prospector Behe in popular cowboy actor John Wayne's TALL IN THE SADDLE (1944). An expensive A-western, Raymond has a happy reunion with scene-stealing George "Gabby" Hayes. Following Brown's camera finish with GHOST GUNS (1944) by early August 1944, the 13th series effort, Brown took a break from the "Nevada Jack McKenzie" horse operas to act in what would be his last drawing-room role. It was Monogram's A-drama FOREVER YOURS (1945) that began shots July 31, 1944. Johnny Mack portrays U. S. Army Major Tex who performs polio research. He is attracted to disease victim Gale Storm, daughter of a society doctor portrayed by distinguish-voiced actor, Conrad Nagel.

Brown went back to the boots-and-saddles grind around mid-September 1944, with GUN SMOKE (1945) as "Nevada Jack McKenzie" in the series 14th B-oater for the unusual choice of Indian grave robbers wanting jewels. On wrapping his 16th Monogram B-Western of STRANGER FROM SANTA FE (1945) near mid-January 1945, Johnny Mack was assigned to a non-studio series B-sagebrusher FLAME OF THE WEST (1945) as peaceful frontier physician John Poore, reluctant to use firearms until he avenges murdered lawman Douglass Dumbrille. Camera work finished here for Brown about mid-February, then giving him a four-month acting break.

Raymond Hatton, meanwhile took advantage of the "McKenzie" production lull by traveling to Columbia Pictures and emoting a cattle-rustler part in cowboy warbler Ken Curtis' RHYTHM ROUND-UP (1945) which cameraed February 24, 1945 – March 12, 1945. Ray next acted in the Monogram A-musical SUN BONNET SUE (1945) as it lensed starting April 23, 1945, until late May 1945. This 89-minute film saw Hatton as an 1890s political candidate inside New York City's Bowery section.

Brown and Hatton resumed on the 17th of their regular features with THE LOST TRAIL (1945) about June 22, 1945. Once BORDER BANDITS (1946), the 19th entry ended work in mid-August 1945, Johnny Mack and Raymond were to take another exit from the series, and appear for cameras on DRIFTING ALONG (1946), done from September 24, 1945, into early October 1945. Johnny Mack's character was as rodeo champ Steve Garner who aids pretty ranchwoman Lynne Carver, pestered by rustlers. There is a hint of romance between Brown and Carver, but none takes place. The opening footage has Johnny Mack singing "Thirsty Trails", but his voice is dubbed while toting a saddle over one shoulder.

Brown and Hatton next did what would be the 20th and final B-entry on the "Nevada Jack McKenzie" series with THE HAUNTED MINE (1946) where they caught gold thieves in lensing that wound by late October 1945. Whatever reason Monogram bigwigs had for terminating these particular features is not known.

Johnny with Joan Woodbury (Monogram, 1946).

But Monogram continued with both Johnny Mack and Raymond under contract. They were, however, to take another two month studio hiatus before cameras proceeded for their new B-Westerns. Each succeeding one was having them portray different-named individuals routing the same type crooks as they did on the "McKenzie" outings. The first, with no assigned series name, was UNDER ARIZONA SKIES (1946) which ended shots toward end of January 1946.

The mostly young female leads for Brown's remaining Monograms into mid-year 1952 were Reno Blair [Reno Browne], Claudia Drake, Christine McIntyre, Jennifer Holt, Jan Bryant, Evelyn Brent, Peggy Wynne, June Harrison, Kay Morley, Virginia Belmont, Virginia Carroll, Mildred Coles, Christine Larson, Evelyn Finley, Gerry Patterson, Felice Ingersoll, Jane Adams, Gail Davis, Lois Hall, Phyllis Coates, Virginia Herrick, Noel Neill, and Barbara Allen.

Raymond Hatton snared a big support role, as he continued the Brown's throughout 1946, with Paramount Pictures portraying the Venango scout on super-producer Cecil B. DeMille's UNCONQUERED (1948). A vast $4.2 million Colonial American drama in Technicolor, DeMille herded this big 1763 screenplay, starring Gary Cooper, before lenses July 29, 1946 – November 8, 1946. Raymond received 29th billing out of a cast of 200.

That wasn't all for Hatton away from Johnny Mack. Monogram's new subsidiary, Allied Artists, was formed as a releasing venue for its more bigger-budgeted productions. An initial $200,000 feature done with Cinecolor lenses for Allied Artists distribution was BLACK GOLD (1947), produced from late November 1946, through late January 1947, which starred Mexican Irish actor Anthony Quinn. Raymond had the part of a horse trainer.

Hatton continued his partnering on the Johnny Mack's throughout 1947 production at Monogram. On July 12, 1948, the first day's shooting for THE SHERIFF OF MEDICINE BOW (1948), Brown and Hatton were joined by new sidekick Max Terhune.

Terhune was a versatile entertainer. He earlier starred with Republic's "The Three Mesquiteers" Westerns series in 21 low-budget B-oater movies done from late August 1936, through late March 1939. Later, Max was "Alibi" Terhune for all 24 B-films with Monogram's "The Range Busters" outings, photoed between early July 1940, and end of June 1943.

Max Terhune gained popularity as the veteran ventriloquist throwing his voice to wooden puppet Elmer. But Terhune was good, as well, in each series with the customary shooting, riding, fighting and other action sequences.

Max Terhune's ability, however, to obtain more sidekick roles greatly slumped once "The Range Busters" ended. But, three months later, he did COWBOY CANTEEN (1944), a Columbia musical B-Western starring Charles Starrett along with other guest stars when the film was before lenses September 21, 1943 – October 4, 1943. And Max corralled a sidekick spot next to oats B-lead Allan Lane for his SHERIFF OF SUNDOWN (1944), in production at end of May 1944. Terhune also snagged parts on two independent sagebrushers, HARMONY TRAIL (1944), Ken Maynard's swan song to B-Westerns and Cal Shrum's SWING, COWBOY, SWING (1944).

But Max really had his biggest film drought from the end of 1944 until early July 1948 obtaining no new film roles except for sidekicking to Republic B-action cowboy singer Monte Hale in ALONG THE OREGON TRAIL (1947), lensed with Trucolor from March 27, 1947 – April 21, 1947.

Then, Max Terhune was emoting once more as he hooked up with Johnny Mack Brown and Raymond Hatton for Monogram's THE SHERIFF OF MEDICINE BOW, dealing with an attempted ranch seizure. Max would be usually cast as a storekeeper with some riding chores, plus an opportunity to converse with puppet Elmer.

Two B-Westerns later, Hatton bade farewell to the Brown gallopers as he finished a long association of over 5-1/2 years with them on HIDDEN DANGER (1948) which wrapped shots by early October 1948.

A different change of pace was in store for Johnny Mack as he paired with rugged A-Western star Rod Cameron on STAMPEDE (1949) for Allied Artists that went about three weeks in shooting before stopping October 26, 1948. In STAMPEDE, Brown played sheriff Aaron Ball mediating settlers' problems.

Johnny Mack followed here with an almost five-month absence from Monogram until studio cameras beckoned him again, this time on April 4, 1949 for WEST OF EL DORADO (1949) He portrays an ex-ranch foreman chasing down stolen bank loot. Brown also has an extended scene alongside juvenile player Teddy Infuhr performing some of his famous gun acrobatics.

Johnny with comic Max Terhune (circa 1948).

Two B-Westerns afterward once WESTERN RENEGADES (1949) was done close to mid-July 1949, Max Terhune departed the Brown movies and Monogram having appeared in nine of them.

For the time being starring on WEST OF WYOMING (1950), produced from September 19, 1949, Johnny Mack was without a regular saddlepal. Brown's sidekick status was to somewhat improve at least once

Max Terhune, Johnny, and Reno Browne/Blair in WEST OF EL DORADO (Monogram, 1949).

for OVER THE BORDER (1950), beginning footage shots January 16, 1950. A tale here necessitated capture of ore thieves. Johnny Mack's partner was old-time actor Milburn Morante who, throughout just about all of the cowboy's Monogram sagebrushers back to 1943, was seen mostly as an old codger, prospector, etc., offering valuable advice to anyone who would listen.

Monogram then took Brown away a second time from his regular B-Western series to co-star once more with A-actioner Rod Cameron on SHORT GRASS (1950) in production August 7, 1950 – August 29, 1950. For this expensive Allied Artists outdoor adventure, Johnny Mack was Marshal Keown in love with female lead Cathy Donns.

Mid-October 1950 was a production end on Brown's COLORADO AMBUSH (1951), with the screenplay done by perennial Monogram bad guy Myron Healey.

A more stable cowboy partner for Johnny Mack was introduced in six of his final seven Monogram films by Spring 1951 as seasoned thespian Jimmy Ellison came on board for OKLAHOMA JUSTICE (1951).

Ellison earlier attained only minor B-Western success starting out on the Hopalong Cassidy series in 1935 as Lucky Jenkins with star William Boyd. Jimmy departed these

Paramount Pictures releases upon finishing eight of them with BORDERLAND (1937) that ended footage duties on December 19, 1936.

Jimmy Ellison was next confined during the late 1930s – late 1940s to B-dramas and comedies for various signed movie companies. He re-entered the hayburner genre with LAST OF THE WILD HORSES (1948), a Screen Guild release filmed in south-western Oregon. Jimmy next launched out by doing what was hoped to be a long movie venture for at least five years as he began shooting six B-sagas on November 7, 1949, for Lippert Pictures release. This "Irish Cowboys" series juxtaposed shooting for every film by doing certain segments together at one time. Thomas Carr did the unusual directing and wound all his productions by late December 1949.

But this series evidently failed at the box office as there were no more extra B-Westerns made by Jimmy "Shamrock" Ellison and pal Russ "Lucky" Hayden.

Ellison's prospects for any new movies, regardless of genre, looked bleak, but he managed to corral budget leads for Columbia's THE TEXAN MEETS CALAMITY JANE (1950) in Cinecolor and I KILLED GERONIMO (1950), an Eagle-Lion release. The single other movie Jimmy did before joining Monogram was in a Lippert B-musical, KENTUCKY JUBILEE (1951) starring funny, big-eyed comic Jerry Colonna.

The roles for Ellison with Brown from movie to movie starting on OKLAHOMA JUSTICE ranged the gamut of stagecoach driver, sheriff, ex-U.S. Calvary officer, gold-mind inheritor, and outlaw's brother. Jimmy then left Johnny Mack upon wrap of DEAD MAN'S TRAIL (1952) around April 1952.

B-Western production was to decline at Monogram Pictures as the year 1952 progressed due to increased competition from the television medium's oats –oriented half-hour shows with Gene Autry, Roy Rogers, The Cisco Kid (Duncan Renaldo), The Lone Ranger (John Hart), and Hopalong Cassidy (William Boyd).

Johnny with Jane "Poni" Adams in OUTLAW GOLD (Monogram, 1950).

Johnny Mack finished his 66th and last Monogram production, CANYON AMBUSH (1952), in June 1952, that had him after a masked rider who causes havoc for area citizens.

It was possibly a combination decision of both Brown and Monogram Pictures that the B-cowboy star not renew his contract, which he successfully maintained for nine years and four months.

Brown after all, was close to 48 years

Pierce Lyden, Johnny, and Jimmy Ellison in WHISTLING HILLS (Monogram, 1951).

old and probably feeling his age what with all the physical dexterity required of him from doing 17 years of B-Westerns that always involved practically endless segments of fisticuffs, riding, and gun shooting.

Many ardent fans of Johnny Mack Brown may not realize this fact about him: He ranked a close No. 2 behind good friend Charles Starrett, Columbia Pictures saddler, in the amount of B-Westerns he made. Starrett did 131, while Brown filmed 110, just five more than B-actioner Bob Steele, No. 3. This was some record for Johnny Mack as there were around 80 other cowboy star actors who made budget oaters as well.

Brown also maintained consistency each year from 1940 through 1950 with his annual ranking as one of the Top Ten Western Box Office Attractions for Motion Picture Herald Poll and Box Office Poll. The latter poll made no star listings for the year 1943.

His Monogram feats now becoming cinema history, Johnny Mack took a 10-month acting break, and then did some March 1953 lensing as one of several guest stars with old-timer Hoot Gibson on THE MARSHAL'S DAUGHTER (1953), a United Artists release. Others joining Brown in a great capacity were Jimmy Wakely, Preston Foster, and Buddy Baer.

Only performing in occasional television shows the next 11-1/2 years, Johnny Mack

Brown had a motion-picture revival of some stature October 9, 1964, as he appeared before camera for a medium-size part with producer Alex Gordon's THE BOUNTY KILLER (1965), an too, a $194,000 A-Western, then later on Gordon's REQUIEM FOR A GUNFIGHTER (1965), which probably had the same-area negative-cost figure. Both features were lensed in Technicolor and widescreen Technicolor with an Embassy Pictures release.

Brown, in familiar company, was amongst past B-Western greats on Alex's two movies that also saw Rod Cameron, Buster Crabbe, Bob Steele, Lane Chandler, and even old ex-Monogram partner Raymond Hatton. Johnny Mack was once more on recognizable lawman turf as Sheriff Green in THE BOUNTY KILLER.

Brown made his final Western before Technicolor/Techniscope lenses on veteran sage lead Rory Calhoun's APACHE UPRISING (1966) photoed from June 14, 1965 – June 25, 1965. A Paramount Pictures distribution for prolific producer A.C. Lyles, the movie had Johnny Mack as Sheriff Ben Hall who became embroiled in a heated argument while talking to female lead Corinne Calvet.

Johnny Mack Brown's number of horse-opera appearances became admired, film achievement. He was, indeed, that soft-spoken, gracious gentleman from southeastern Alabama so revered by his many daring exploits on the silver screen.

Johnny, Christine McIntyre, and Jack Ingram in CANYON AMBUSH (Monogram, 1952). This was Johnny's last starring film.

THEY'RE WRITING ABOUT JOHNNY

William C. Russell (article in *The Old Cowboy Picture Show*): Johnny Mack Brown was one of the greatest and would probably get the vote as the best all-around cowboy star to come out of the Hollywood corral. While other Western heroes were noted for a particular trait that set them apart from other sagebrush heroes, Johnny excelled in all departments. He was, for example, a heck-of-a fighter and many of his movies contain some of the toughest fisticuffs on film. He was no slouch when it came to riding either, was quick with his six-shooter and was a better than average actor who delivered lines without hesitation. In fact, his deep southern accent added a unique quality that set him apart from other Western actors, save maybe Randolph Scott, that other Southern gentleman.

Johnny Mack Brown was an A-Westerner who rode the B-Western range. Like several other Western stars of equal talents and skills, Brown could easily have made it as a main-feature Western star. And, in a way, we B-Western fans are not sorry he didn't make it. We enjoyed his dazzling action on the screen each Saturday and his absence from that genre would have left a great void. The Monogram Westerns found Johnny at his peak. While some were not quite as good as others, lacking in action and plot format, the production was always good and Johnny carried them through with ease. He was such an easygoing, likeable Western star that his performances were always tops. Even the worst of the Monograms were good, thanks in large part to Brown.

John Brooker (Brooker interviewed Johnny in November 1970): My wife and I met him in a bar near his home in Parklabrea Apartments on South Burnside Los Angeles in November 1970. I called his agency on Ventura to arrange the meeting and he was more than happy to see us. He was the perfect Southern gentleman all evening. Many people stopped at our table to say hello to Johnny, and he would call them Sir or Ma'am if he didn't know them. He was a most polite and gentle host.

When Johnny got to his feet to say goodbye, he said he would be staying on in the bar. I guessed it would be for a few more drinks with his friends, but he was a most gracious host for us and drank very little while he was with us. But I did recall what Marshall Reed said to us, "Johnny was getting a bit heavy towards the end. He liked his drink and Southern cooking."

The following quotes were made by Johnny at that meeting. "In 1930, after 2-3 years of 'indoor' dramas and comedies, MGM put me in a Western, BILLY THE KID with Wally

Beery as Pat Garrett. William S. Hart worked as an adviser on it. I learned a lot from him and we became good friends. I did the GREAT MEADOW, another outdoor picture a year or so later, and then made a couple more Westerns for other studios. They obviously thought I was more suited to Westerns and I was offered a serial with Wally Beery's brother, Noah, and Noah's son. Then one at Universal, but it was a far cry from MGM. I had worked with Garbo, Pickford and Crawford at MGM.

"The Supreme Westerns were the low point of my career; they were very cheap, just thrown together. They weren't very good. I did a couple of years with Hackel, then more serials at Universal, and they signed me

(Regarding the studios teaming of cowboy stars):" I don't think any of us found it ideal, but musical Westerns were popular and Universal wanted singing in my pictures. I did six with Bob Baker before doing some solo, and another seven with Tex Ritter. My sidekick was Fuzzy Knight—a naturally funny man. We made 28 together. When the Universal series ended, I went to Monogram. I was there almost 10 years. Ray Hatton was my sidekick. He was a wonderful guy to work with.

"Monogram put me in two bigger Westerns with Rod Cameron before my series finished. Did you ever hear of a man called Ken Murray? He was making a film with Hoot Gibson and was having a job with the money and selling the idea. I did a card game scene for him. I think he sold it (the film was THE MARSHAL'S DAUGHTER, and according to Jimmy Wakely who was also in the movie, neither he nor Johnny got paid for their work).

(Regarding making APACHE UPRISING): "I enjoyed making that one. I thought I might be offered something else but nothing good has come along since then. I liked making Westerns; it was fun. I worked with so many nice people, and if I had to do it all over again, I wouldn't change it."

Don Cotterman (1973 article in *Horse and Rider* magazine): Johnny's performances were stalwart, both as an actor and one who could perform feats of agility with convincing realism. The only use of stuntmen was imposed as a matter of studio preference. Brown recalls that Cliff Lyons and Yakima Canutt were among the men who took over when the script would call for something that required someone whose expertise was directed toward the performance of stunts that would have been suicidal for anyone else.

Throughout his career Brown demonstrated a vigor and enthusiasm that seemed incongruous to his quiet manner. When he was not working on a picture he undertook extensive personal appearance tours. There were rodeo appearances and countless in-person contacts with millions of fans or theater chain tours throughout the country. During WW II he sold bonds while on tour for the government to help bring victory to the Allies.

Buck Rainey (*Heroes of the Range*): One of the few stars to be honored with a star implanted on Hollywood Boulevard, Johnny Mack Brown has a secure place in the hearts and minds of thousand of movie fans who remembered the good old days when he and Rebel, his faithful steed, rode the Hollywood range. That's almost as good as a kiss from the lovely lass at the fadeout, and much longer lasting.

Leonard Maltin (author and film critic): Although Brown was a capable actor, it was his athletic abilities that made him a Saturday-matinee favorite; stuntmen agreed that he "threw the best punch in pictures," and he never failed to bring down the house with his frequent displays of expert gun twirling.

Alan Barbour (*Saturday Afternoon at the Movies*): As a Western star he was one of the most convincing of the breed. When he threw a fake punch he gave it every thing he had, convincing the audience that he really was connecting.

Doug Bruton (a fan): When I lived in Lubbock, Texas, Johnny's brother had a men's clothing store there. I often went into the store to talk about Johnny—one of my all time favorite Western stars. His brother sounded just like Johnny Mack, and if you didn't look at him, it was as if Johnny was in the same room with you.

I had the opportunity to talk with Johnny on the phone, about two months prior to his passing, and it was a real thrill for me. I was overwhelmed. I had become pretty good friends with his brother and I was really surprised when he handed me the phone and there was that great Alabama sound on the other end of the line.

At that time Lubbock was hosting the College All-American football game and Johnny was scheduled to be the guest of honor at the upcoming game. I told him he had brought me so many hours of thrills and adventure and that I was looking forward to seeing him at the game. He thanked me for being a fan and admirer. He never made it to the game. He passed away a couple of months later. I was told by his brother that Johnny was a Christian Scientist and did not seek medical attention until the latter stages of some type of kidney problem.

If I had been told back in the 1940s that I would one day talk with Johnny Mack Brown, I would never have believed it. Talking to Johnny was a thrill I will never forget.

Hans J. Wollstein (author): Johnny Mack Brown once starred opposite Greta Garbo, a distinction no other B-Western hero could claim. But M-G-M, who had him under contract in those tumultuous early days of sound films, didn't keep him around solely because he was so darn good-looking. He never failed to deliver fine and extremely natural performances, an ability that stood him in good stead in his later career as a cowboy hero.

Along with John Wayne and Bob Steele, Johnny Mack was probably the best actor among his peers. Not that his particular genre demanded all that much thespian talents from its practitioners, but he never seemed to be slumming no matter how trite a character or plot. Johnny Mack Brown, it was obvious, loved what he was doing and apparently never regretted leaving mainstream Hollywood behind for the rough-and-tumble world of B-Western production.

Don Miller (*Hollywood Corral*): The latter years of his Western starring series had been mostly downhill, but he had outlasted most of the cowboy regulars. Completely in character, he departed quietly, and without fanfare, and with style.

A macho-looking Johnny in THREE ON A HONEYMOON (Fox, 1934). Charles Starrett was also in the film.

THE FANS SPEAK

(Author's Note: I have asked several friends, who are knowledgeable B-Westerns fans, to give their thoughts on Johnny and his movies).

Paul Dellinger (author of many Western and serial articles): I'm not sure which of Johnny Mack Brown's movies is the first one I ever saw, but I know it was one of his Monogram series and that Raymond "Sandy" Hatton was his co-star. The year was probably 1945, when I began what became a weekly ritual of going to the Friday night double-feature in my hometown theater. The ending of the movie saddened me. It ended with Johnny and "Sandy" saying goodbye to the entourage of people with whom they had just shared a great adventure, and then, as they rode away, Johnny and Sandy took separate trails and waved farewell to one another. I was unhappy at the thought that, after what all these people had gone through together, they would never see each other again.

All of which shows how unsophisticated I was in the ways of B-Westerns, that riding into the sunset was never forever, and the same cast of characters would be back in another adventure before we knew it. In fact, it would not be until I was fully grown and ran into the revival of interest in the B-Westerns which, for me, began in the 1970s, that I understood the genesis of the cowboys taking separate trails. Raymond Hatton, along with Tim McCoy and Buck Jones, had been in Monogram's "Rough Riders" series, of which I'd never heard as a kid. At the end of every movie, they would ride off separately to different states.

With McCoy dropping out of the series and Jones' tragic death in a nightclub fire, only Hatton was left to carry on. He continued his role of "Sandy Hopkins" with a new leading man, Brown, initially playing "Nevada Jack" McKenzie (so Johnny would ride off to Nevada at the end of each movie and Sandy to Texas).

I'm sure Johnny had moved on from his "Nevada Jack" persona by the time I began enjoying his movies, generally playing a different character in each picture. But he still cut a striking figure, astride his palomino, Rebel, alongside Hatton's paint horse, Lucky. And I got the impression that Johnny and Raymond Hatton turned out their Monogram product more quickly than their counterparts at Republic and Columbia, mainly because Johnny was the only star I would watch one week only to see a preview of one of his movies coming next week as well. It happened twice during my decade of B-Western movie-viewing.

There was a time when B-Westerns were fading away and television was rustling audiences for low-budget Westerns when I saw a Johnny Mack Brown advertised on TV. Imagine my confusion when I saw him dressed all in black, riding a white horse, wearing two guns and without Raymond Hatton. It was one of his earlier Universal's, of course.

Again, it would take the B-Western revival during my adulthood to teach me about his series at Universal co-starring with Tex Ritter (whom I remembered, before that, only from his "Texas Rangers" series at PRC), and his still earlier solo efforts at Universal, Republic and Supreme, and even a few Westerns at places like Paramount and MGM), not to mention his still-earlier non-western romantic leads opposite some of the top female stars of the 1930. All of that history eluded me when I was looking forward to his next Monogram Western.

Later, in the 1960s, there would come a time when I would see him in less flattering roles in a couple movies that gathered together stars from bygone days for hardly more than cameos. I didn't even recognize him at first, as a bartender in REQUIEM FOR A GUNFIGHTER (1965, Embassy) starring Rod Cameron as the hero and Stephen McNally as the villain, and a cast which included Tim McCoy, Bob Steele, Lane Chandler, Dick Jones, Rand Brooks, and even Raymond Hatton! It was my wife who spotted him first, more by his Southern-accented voice, I think, than his appearance. Still, even in a small supporting role, and even as a mere bartender, it is Johnny Mack Brown who shoots the gun out of McNally's hand during a crucial moment at the climax.

His roles in the other two movies with conglomerations of former Western movie stars were even less flattering, as was a role I saw him in on Raymond Burr's "Perry Mason" TV series, as a character which even he, in the courtroom finale, admitted was less than a gentleman. At least he wasn't the murderer. And he did have the good judgment to be the husband of Marie Windsor. Then there was his appearance, in what really was just a cameo, in THE MARSHAL'S DAUGHTER, a movie produced by comedian Ken Murray in 1953 which somehow had the look of a much older picture. And that was a year after what I see in retrospect was Johnny's last Monogram Western.

Then there was his appearance at a couple of Allied Artist features, both in support of Rod Cameron: STAMPEDE (1949), which I would eventually see on TV, and SHORT GRASS (1950), which played at the first-run theater in my hometown rather than the little B-movie weekend house. That was in the days when movie theaters advertised scenes with photographs from the pictures on the outside, and I walked by the "main" theater several times that week, before I actually saw the movie, to see Johnny Mack Brown in what seemed unfamiliar clothing, sporting a sheriff's badge on his vest, and looking forward to seeing how he would acquit himself in somebody else's picture. His characters, both times, acquitted themselves just fine, even if it was Cameron would get the girl each time. Even the Monograms went downhill somewhat toward the end of their run, which went from 1943 through 1952.

Although Max "Alibi" Terhune and his ventriloquist dummy, Elmer Sneezeweed, had been popular in earlier trio Westerns, I found it not an improvement when he appeared alongside, and then replaced, Raymond Hatton in the sidekick role. Hatton was a very good actor, like George "Gabby" Hayes, above and beyond the traditional sidekick. Terhune somehow seemed less competent. And eventually even Terhune went away and, for four Monograms toward the end of their run, the studio teamed up Johnny with a younger sidekick, none other than Jimmy Ellison who (I would later learn) had cut his cowboy teeth as the first youthful "Hopalong Cassidy" sidekick.

I had seen Ellison several times over the years, as Buffalo Bill in the re-release of Gary Cooper's take on Wild Bill Hickok in Cecil B. DeMille's THE PLAINSMAN, in the one-shot "LAST OF THE WILD HORSES (which inexplicably played as the second feature in my hometown theater, the slot usually going to a B-mystery or Bowery Boys comedy), and in a six-pack of hastily-produced B-Westerns with another former Hoppy sidekick, Russell Hayden, and Raymond Hatton, and Fuzzy Knight (who had been an earlier comic sidekick for Johnny at Universal), not to mention the future Julie Adams.

Finally, Monogram simply had Johnny going it alone, as in CANYON AMBUSH (1952), the last of his Monogram series. Of course, when I was watching it, I didn't know it would be the end of the trail. But Johnny seemed almost a reluctant hero in it, someone who almost had to be pushed into combating the outlawry (although there was a neat trick of him using a mirror in front of a window to reflect himself when he was marked for being ambushed).

But as long as I live, I will remember Johnny in that decade of Monogram pictures, riding Rebel and doing amazing twirls and tosses with his stag-handled pistol, finishing off the bad guy in a fight by placing one hand behind the bad guy's head and smashing his other fist into the baddie's face, and his gentle Alabama accent in which he would pronounce the word "sheriff" like "sher-eef," and the Monogram background action music (also used for Jimmy Wakely and Whip Wilson, the other parts of the Monogram trio).

Sometimes Johnny seemed more leisurely and less intense than his counterparts at other studios, but he was always worth spending an hour of viewing time with.

Jim Hamby (a fan who has attended many Western film festivals): Most fans agree that Johnny's best features were the ones he made for Universal from 1939 to 1943. The pictures he made during this period with Tex Ritter and Bob Baker were especially enjoyable. I saw a few of these movies as a young boy but did not remember much about them. I now have most of these movies in my personal collection and have watched them numerous times over the years. I do remember the Monogram pictures Johnny made in the 1940s and early 1950s. Monogram must have been given their best scripts to Johnny, and he always had a good cast of supporting actors.

Since 1980, when I began attending the film festivals, I have seen most of the films that Johnny made for Supreme. These movies also have some good plots.

Many of Johnny's Monogram pictures were filmed at the Walker/Monogram Ranch, a place that I have visited twice while in California. I always enjoy seeing movies filmed at this location.

I had the opportunity to see Johnny Mack Brown, in the late 1940s, when he appeared at the Liberty Theatre in my home town of North Wilkesboro, North Carolina. It was a little after 5:00 in the afternoon, when Johnny had finished one of his stage shows, that he put his guns behind the curtains of the theatre and walked across the street to the Princess Cafe to dine. When he returned from the restaurant, he discovered the guns had been stolen. He had to do his next two shows without the guns. Since gun-twirling had been an important part of his act, he was forced to improvise. Johnny was not normally a two-gun man, but he was using two guns for his stage act. Johnny is one of my favorite cowboy actors of the B-Western era.

Bill Sasser (Williamsburg Film Festival Promoter): Johnny Mack Brown must rate with the all-time cowboy greats. I thoroughly enjoyed all the series work that he did. My favorite, of course, are the Universals. THE SILVER BULLET is one of the best Westerns ever made. His co-starring films with Tex Ritter are top rate. I also enjoyed his Monogram adventures. He was an expert gun handler, a fine actor and a great action star. If you could only choose one action hero to have a collection of Westerns of, I would highly recommend Johnny Mack Brown.

Doug Morris (newspaper editor): For those of us who grew up feeling the powder of a dirt road between our toes, Johnny Mack Brown was one of us. He had three names, he had an accent, he had manners, and he had that Southern spirit. He was a cowboy hero, and he was homefolk.

When he rode onto the silver screen in 1930, it was the beginning of over 100 films. And when he rode his last around 1952, the only thing changed about Johnny Mack Brown was his horse. My memory of him is mostly in his later works, like WHISTLING HILLS, OKLAHOMA JUSTICE, and MAN FROM SONORA, all around 1951. Many fans can cite different films as their favorites. Really, I liked them all. They all seemed to be actually happening just outside our window.

In a Supreme Studio film, Johnny Mack Brown wore a black hat, but he was still the good guy. And, he KISSED the leading lady. But we forgave him of that when we kids became older and learned fireworks exist in more than bullets.

Johnny Mack Brown brought Southern grace and charm to a corral of cowboys. He ranked behind Gene Autry, Roy Rogers, Hopalong Cassidy, and Bill Elliott. One of the top five's not bad for a country boy. He was one of us, and he made us proud.

Tinsley Yarbrough (author): As a fellow Alabamian and alumnus of the University of Alabama's "Million Dollar Band," I have always had a warm spot in my heart for Johnny Mack Brown, a true Southern gentleman if ever there was one. Co-workers sometimes complain privately about certain stars, but never about Johnny Mack. For him, they only have words of praise and affection.

When I was an Alabama student in the early sixties, Johnny Mack attended at least one of the Crimson Tide football games, seemingly enjoying the adulation heaped on the former gridiron as well as celluloid star. He was a lot heavier than in his movie days, his face fairly puffy. But he still had that wonderful smile!

By 1985, when I made my first trip to California, Johnny Mack was with the angels. One night, though, a group of us went to the Tail of the Cock supper club on Ventura Boulevard, where he had served as host toward the end. An elderly waiter remembered him fondly. Apparently, Johnny Mack had difficulty remembering at what tables he seated parties. One night, there was a fire in the restaurant. Patrons and staff were evacuated and the fire alarm rung. Firemen quickly arrived and put out the fire. But while standing outside waiting for permission to return to the premises, staffers began asking where Johnny Mack was. Finally, they found him in a back booth of the restaurant, calmly nursing a drink. Our cowboy hero had nerves of steel! God bless, Johnny Mack.

Grady Franklin (former publisher of *The Western Film*): Johnny Mack was like a brother to me. When I was a mere boy back in the 30s I was not lucky enough to see Johnny Mack Brown on the silver screen. I was born in 1929 in upper East Tennessee and the five or 10 cents it cost to see a Western at the Grand or Ritz Theater in Elizabethton was not easy to come by. Besides, even those few pennies were needed by our less than affluent family to help provide life's essentials during the great depression.

So, not until much later would I be able to enjoy Johnny Mack's 1930 classic, BILLY THE KID, or any of the fine westerns he did for Supreme, Universal and Monogram. Nor would I see his action-packed serials until my adult life at the various film festivals, and via videotape. But once I discovered Johnny Mack Brown, he was one of my absolute favorites. I bonded with him especially during World War II because he reminded me of my older brother, Millard, who was serving in the Navy.

Johnny on tour.

Because Tex Ritter was also one of my favorites, I really enjoyed the features he made with Johnny Mack. There they were, two of my heroes on the screen together. It was almost too good to be true for a youngster trying to find his way into adulthood.

Pretty much during the entire film career of Johnny Mack Brown my dad, Roby Franklin, was a commercial photographer in East Tennessee and Western North Carolina. He had a studio at one time or another in the Tennessee towns of Elizabethton, Roan Mountain, Mountain City, and in Spruce Pine, North Carolina.

I didn't realize until recently (the summer of 2004) that my sister, Ruby, had saved many of the B&W negatives from my dad's collection. When she passed away some of the negatives were sent to me for evaluation. That's how we happen to be looking at the accompanying photo of Johnny Mack Brown. I doubt that it was published previously. Also, I have no idea when or exactly where it was taken. I suspect that the film star was on a personal appearance tour in the area and my dad made the photo in one of the aforementioned towns.

I don't recall my dad coming home one day and saying, "I shot a picture of Johnny Mack Brown today." But, I can tell by looking at the negative that it was his work.

There was a story going around during my youth that a truck hauling Ken Maynard's famous horse, Tarzan, had wrecked somewhere along U.S. 19E near Hampton. I never saw a picture of that mishap nor did I know if the Western star was in the area at the time. In my later life I would become a news photographer and, as such, it would have been Old Grady who would have taken such a photograph, had that area been his news beat.

I'm sure other film stars passed through East Tennessee during those years but I have no documentation. I do recall watching a Jack Randall Western at Valley Forge Elementary School in the late 30s, but no personal appearance with the screening. And, sometime during the war, Robert Taylor made a train stop as close as nearby Johnson City. The only "stars" I met in those days, back in those Tennessee hills, was when I was an usher at the Bonnie Kate and Ritz Theaters in Elizabethton. Country singer Cowboy Copas appeared on stage at the Bonnie Kate as did the Three Stooges but, alas, no Roy Rogers, Tex Ritter or Gene Autry.

However, life seems to be fair after all. As an adult, after a successful career in journalism and public relations, it was a pure joy for me to attend Western film festivals in the 80s and 90s. During that time I was editor and publisher of the *Western Film Newsletter*, and had the good fortune to writes stories and make pictures for such publications as *The Big Reel*, *Classic Images*, *Under Western Skies,* and *Favorite Westerns*.

So, old Grady leaves you with this thought: If things aren't going right in your life, stick around awhile because chances are they will get better.

POSTHUMOUS AWARDS

Lachlan "Locky" Brown's acceptance speech for Johnny's 2000 induction into the Rose Bowl Hall of Fame

Thank you. Thank you very much; it is indeed a great honor for me to accept this prestigious award which is being presented to my father today on his induction into the Rose Bowl Hall of Fame.

I and my sisters, my family members and one of my father's sisters who are here with us today are all deeply appreciative of this recognition.

In 1957, when Dad was inducted into the National Football Collegiate Hall of Fame I was fortunate to have been stationed in the Navy at Pensacola, Florida and attended that ceremony at the University of Alabama in Tuscaloosa. The ceremony was at halftime, during which dad made a beautiful acceptance speech. I can't recall all that he said, but I do remember the tribute and recognition given to his teammates who collectively made his success possible. I certainly know that were he here today to accept this award, he would again give credit to his teammates, his coach Wallace Wade and, as well, two other players. I know dad would single out Pooley Hubert, the old man of the team at age 21 they called Papa Pooley, who was key to Alabama's 20 to 19 victory over the University of Washington Huskies, and to the great Washington player

Johnny was inducted into the Rose Bowl Hall of Fame in 2000. Several members of his family were on hand for the celebration. Pictured left to right: Cynthia (daughter), Lachlan (son), Christopher (grandson), and Chris (great-grandson). Photo courtesy of the Pasadena Tournament of Roses Committee)

and powerhouse George Wilson. That 1926 Rose Bowl game can not be discussed without mentioning and giving credit to those two great athletes.

Also, I would be remiss if I didn't mention one of dad's biggest supporters — my mother. She was one of the University of Alabama's female sponsors, much as the Rose Bowl princesses are today. At age 19, she took the long four day train ride from Tuscaloosa to Pasadena in support of the team, accompanied by University administrators and President Dr. Denny.

So, in conclusion, I would like to thank the Tournament of Roses' nomination and selection committees for this honor which is being bestowed upon my father. His participation in the Rose Bowl was a significant factor in his life and career and I know that this tribute, were dad here today to accept it, would provide great satisfaction and feelings of accomplishment to him as it does for me to accept this award in his behalf. So thank you, thank you very much from my father and all his family.

Locky Brown and Cynthia Brown Hale's acceptance speech for Johnny's Golden Boot Award (2004)

Good evening. I am Locky Brown and I am very pleased to be here with you this evening to recognize and honor my father, John Mack Brown.

I know this recognition of his career would gratify him greatly as so much emphasis has previously been placed on his collegiate football career with his induction into the National Collegiate Football Hall of Fame, State of Alabama Sports Hall of Fame, Helms Athletic Hall of Fame, and, in 2000, the Rose Bowl Hall of Fame. Most recently, in March of this year, dad was inducted into the Alabama Stage and Screen Hall of Fame. So you can see that this Golden Boot recognition of his lifetime effort in films, more specifically Western films, which brought him to the attention of the Americans as well as the worldwide general public, would please him greatly, as it does his family.

Now, since this is a family occasion, I'd like to present my sister Cynthia, who was the real ham in our family while we were growing up. But before doing that, I'd like to mention my two other sisters who would loved to have been here this evening. Unfortunately my older sister Jane is no longer with us and my youngest sister, Sally, lives with her family in Norway. This is an occasion they both would have cherished. But Cynthia is here. She was the extrovert. Dad had a Western suit, hat, boots, a whole

Johnny was inducted into the Alabama Stage and Screen Hall of Fame in March 2004. Johnny's children, Locky and Cynthia, were there to accept the award on Johnny's behalf.

identical outfit similar to his tailored for her at about the age of seven for publicity shoots which she loved doing and did for several years. Now I'd like to introduce Cynthia to say a few words.

Cynthia: *I would just like to add that this Sept. 1st would have been Dad's 100th birthday, so receiving the Golden Boot Award is especially meaningful to the Brown Family, and we thank The Golden Boot Committee for this recognition. As Locky mentioned, Dad got his first taste of fame during his football years at the University of Alabama. The Rose Bowl game of 1926 that he played in is still today considered one of the most important games in Alabama and Rose Bowl history. At MGM, Dad became a leading man to Mary Pickford, Greta Garbo, Mae West, Norma Shearer, Joan Crawford, and later with lovely ladies such as Lois Hall, Noel Neill, and Gale Storm, who are also being honored here tonight. When Dad made BILLY THE KID in 1930, it seemed to be a turning point in his career, from a leading man to the All-American Western Cowboy hero.*

Dad made movies for a variety of studios, but the movies he made at Universal were considered his best. After his contract was up he moved on to Monogram, where he made six to eight movies per year. In all, he made 168 movies, and out of those 131 were Westerns.

Dad passed away in 1974, 30 years ago, but he still had a pretty good year past year. He was honored at Jim Robert's Round-up last August at the Sportsman's Lodge, he was the first inducted to the World Gun Spinners Hall of Fame last September, and as my brother mentioned, we were privileged to receive The State of Alabama's Stage & Screen Hall of Fame Award for him this past March. Now tonight he has received a "gift", the coveted *Golden Boot Award, and we are thrilled and just want to shout, "Congratulations and happy birthday Dad!!!!! We Love you!!!"*

Cynthia and Locky accept Johnny's Golden Boot Award in 2004.

Letter from the Gun Spinning Hall of Fame (2003)

By Mike Chew

Johnny Mack pioneered gun spinning on the silver screen. His ability to manipulate the peacemaker, especially with maneuvers in the air from hand to hand (border shift) took athleticism to a new level. Our Hall of Fame is meant to represent those that have made significant contributions to the sport of gun spinning with Johnny Mack Brown, our first inductee, leading the way and representing those from the silver screen. Other inductees represent categories like Wild West Shows, inventors of gun spinning moves, technical advancees, judges, gun handling coaches, etc.

The Hall is located at the Homestead complex off I-55 S. in Divernon, Illinois, and is meant to honor those more famous—like Johnny—to the lesser known performers. Our goal is to recognize those across the board that are role models for the youth of our sport to the young at heart.

Johnny was the fastest draws in Hollywood.

Dothan honor's hometown hero

To celebrate the 100th year of Johnny's birth, The Dothan, Alabama City Commission issued a proclamation declaring September 1, 2004, as Johnny Mack Brown Day. There was also a cake cutting, a display of memorabilia items, and the showing of THE LONE STAR TRAIL.

The Commission is planning a Johnny Mack Brown Film Festival for 2005. In addition, a committee is working on renaming a street after Johnny, and creating a historic marker.

REVERIES FROM CYNTHIA

By Cynthia Brown Hale (Johnny's daughter)

When asked to look back at home life with Johnny Mack Brown, what seems to surface in my mind are the routine things. Yes, he had to rise early every morning before I did, get to the studio and come home sometimes late after I had been put to bed, but what I remember most were the Sundays that the "men" got together to play tennis on our court all day. Usually, a group of six to twelve that played, and friends would drop by to chat and observe.

Mother's group of women also played on Wednesdays, followed by a luncheon and whatever card game was the rage of the day. Both group's routines lasted for over 25 years on our court and in our home.

Johnny and daughter Cynthia in look-alike costumes (circa 1947).

Once a year parties with guests numbering over 100 were moments I personally relished. I loved greeting people at the front door and I was always allowed to serve my own tray of hors d'oeuvres even when I was only four or five years old. Being able to participate at my small size in the "conga line," as mother led it through the house with dad attached at the tail end, was great fun with a lasting impression.

Mom and dad were great dancers and everyone loved taking turns dancing with them, especially at our young adult parties as we were growing up. All the girls loved to "cut-a-rug" with dad and he was accommodating and made them all look good.

We kids all had our share of dancing lessons from the time we were nine years old through our senior year in high school. Mom and dad were good "jitter-buggers" and taught us a variety of dances, our favorite being the "Boogie Woogie."

Dad would routinely go on personal appearance tours and be gone for months at a time it seemed. During World War II he donated his time to raising money for war bonds through radio shows as well as the tours and he visited many of the hospitals that had wounded, which was always a moving experience. Even mom did her patriotic bit volunteering her time to the USO and the Hollywood Canteen.

They both were there for the important moments in their children's lives like plays, special holiday presentations, talent shows, graduations, tennis matches, football games, etc. Dad always made a point of being available for my father-daughter special days sponsored by the high school and university in Arizona. They also flew back to the University of Alabama, their alma mater, to see oldest daughter Jane, for special occasions. They visited to see Locky play football at Kentucky, when 'Bear' Bryant was coach. Sally, who is the youngest, made it easier by going to universities in California.

Regular visits to the Coliseum for football games were always a treat because dad had a lot of fans not only for his movies, but for his football prowess. Early on he had received recognition from the Helms Football Foundation's Hall of Fame, later to be followed by the National Collegiate Football Hall of Fame Award in 1957. I remember answering the phone when sports writer and long time friend Braven Dyer called to inform him of his acceptance into the Hall.

Dad was presented the award at half time during the homecoming game at his alma mater, the University of Alabama. My brother Locky, who was in Pensacola at the time, was flown up to be there for the ceremonies. A few years later dad was the first to be inducted in to the State of Alabama's Football Hall of Fame (along with his longtime friend Paul 'Bear' Bryant and other sports greats such as Don Hutson and Joe Louis). More recently, in December of 2000, he was one of two to be inducted that year into the Pasadena Rose Bowl's Football Hall of Fame, for Alabama's history making win in 1926. Our family was invited to participate in the many special functions the Rose Bowl sponsored. My brother Locky received the trophy in dad's place, and gave the acceptance speech at the awards luncheon.

Dad and Locky enjoyed duck and pheasant hunting as well as skeet shooting and fishing together, but traditionally dad's men friends took him duck hunting around his birthday September first. That was always a fun event for him and the kids always anticipated the return of the bounty, however for me my excitement tempered to sadness when I saw how pretty some of the ducks were. I always enjoyed eating the duck and wild rice dinner in spite of my mixed feelings. Notable sportsmen Dad enjoyed the company of included Charlie Starrett, 'Big Boy'

Johnny and Connie with daughters Sally and Cynthia, work on the landscaping (circa 1951).

Locky and Johnny get in some football practice.

Guinn Williams, Clark Gable, Rod Cameron, and Charlie Farrell (for tennis).

Dad's polo years were before my time, although I wish I could have been there to see them. The longtime famous Polo Lounge at the Beverly Hills Hotel was named so because that is where dad and his polo buddies hung out after playing at Will Roger's home, the Uplifters, and the Riviera Country Club's polo grounds. Johnny Mack, Will Rogers, Spencer Tracy and Leslie Howard made up a winning team in the early '30s. We have 16mm films you would not believe, of the movie stars that came out to watch the polo matches. Their handsome and beautiful faces are all captured while they were in their prime on our home movies. Two of the most excellent players were, 'Big Boy' Williams and Hal Roach, best known for the "Our Gang" comedies he produced.

There were multitudes of special moments in Johnny Mack Brown's life, with close friends and family as well as with his fans and the public at large. Mom always said she was very grateful for all the wonderful documentation that publicity of Dad, being a motion picture and football star, provided the family through the years.

Long time and dear actor/friend of the family's William Bakewell, in his book *Hollywood Be Thy Name*, describes Johnny Mack as ". . . a Southern gentleman to the core; the embodiment of the clean-cut best in our country's manhood; an all-American nice guy in every respect." On that hard-to-beat note I end my reverie.

(Cynthia later added the following): Dad was a Christian Scientist as was the whole family, but not as an "official member." He was also a drinker and a smoker, which he had acquired prior to his association with the Church. None of the rest of us drank or smoked. Mom & Dad were Baptists and Methodists in Alabama, before coming to California. It was "America's Sweetheart," Mary Pickford, who introduced them to Christian Science.

In reality, we went to church regularly, Dad only occasionally, mainly because of his heavy studio schedule, which got him up early in the morning and home sometimes after dinner. He liked to sleep in on the weekends and play tennis on our court, with his men's tennis group on Sundays. He attended church, when he had some breathing room in his schedule, and always on Easter, Thanksgiving and Christmas.

JOHNNY IN THE POLLS

Popularity Rankings of Johnny Mack Brown		
Year	Motion Picture Herald Poll Ranking	Boxoffice Poll Ranking
1940	6th	9th
1941	7th	8th
1942	6th	8th
1943	5th	No Poll
1944	6th	6th
1945	6th	6th
1946	7th	7th
1947	8th	7th
1948	8th	9th
1949	8th	9th
1950	8th	10th

COMIC BOOKS

(Thanks to Lansing Sexton and Chuck Anderson)

Johnny Mack Brown's first comic book appearance coincided with Tim McCoy's last appearance in *Tim McCoy Western Movie Stories* #21, dated August 1949, and published by Charlton Comics. According to Bob Overstreet's indispensable Comic Book Price Guide, Johnny's own series began in March 1950, as part of Dell Publishing's Four Color anthology series, and continued until February 1959. There were a total of 22 issues in that period, all with photo covers. Some had photo back covers as well.

Johnny also appeared in the first 21 issues of the Dell giant series *Western Roundup* beginning in June 1952, which featured Johnny along with Gene Autry, Roy Rogers, Wild Bill Elliott and Rex Allen. The first nine covers are illustrated in Ernst and Mary Gerber's wonderful Photo-Journal Guide to Comic Books. All nine covers have photo head shots of the five stars with Roy's and Gene's always slightly larger than the others. The first 14 issues also have photo back covers, as do issues 16 and 18, according to Overstreet.

Johnny's first and only other comic venture was in 1939 in issues 4, 5 and 6 of National Periodicals short-lived (six issues) *Movie Comics*. They contain a 3-part adaptation of the serial THE OREGON TRAIL.

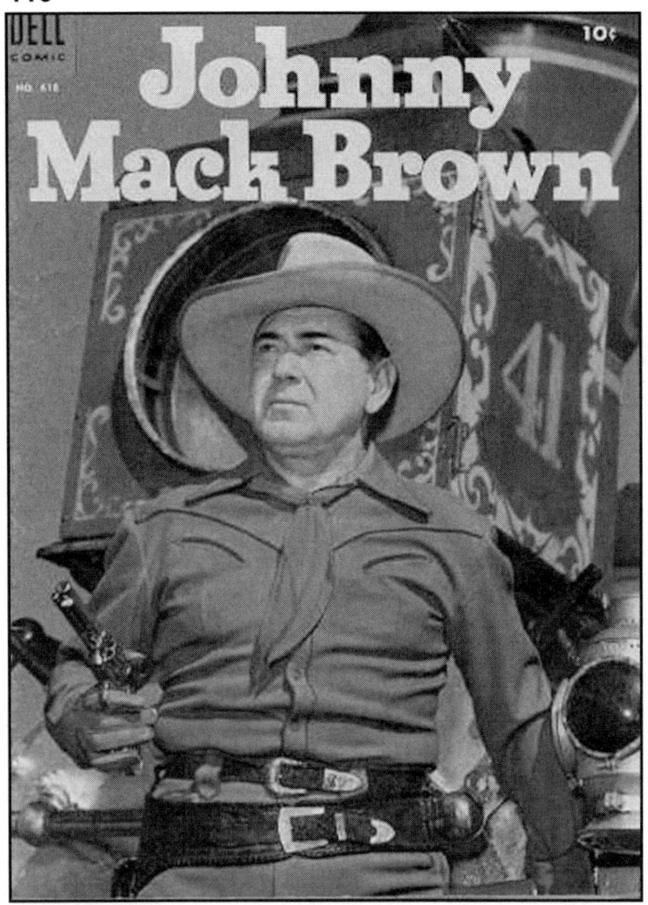
DELL COMIC
10¢
Johnny
Mack Brown

DELL
Still 10¢
Johnny
Mack Brown
He fought for the law...
with both fists!

DELL
10¢
Johnny
Mack Brown
IMPORTANT SEE
DELL'S PLEDGE TO PARENTS
ON INSIDE FRONT COVER

DELL COMIC
10¢
Johnny
Mack Brown

JOHNNY MACK BROWN TIME LINE

September 1, 1904 .... Born in Dothan, Alabama.
May 1922 .... Graduated from Dothan High School.
September 1, 1922 .... Entered the University of Alabama.
January 1, 1926 .... Led Alabama to victory in the Rose Bowl.
June 9, 1926 .... Married Cornelia "Connie" Foster (born 12/4/06).
March 1927 .... 1st appearance on screen (SLIDE, KELLY, SLIDE).
January 1928 .... DIVINE WOMAN released with Greta Garbo.
September 1928 .... 1st sound film, OUR DANCING DAUGHTER, released with Joan Crawford.
December 1928 .... A WOMAN OF AFFAIRS released with Greta Garbo.
April 1929 .... COQUETTE released with Mary Pickford.
July 1929 .... SINGLE STANDARD released with Greta Garbo.
July 9, 1929 .... Daughter, Jane Harriet Brown, born.
March 1930 .... MONTANA MOON released with Joan Crawford.
October 18, 1930 .... BILLY THE KID released.
May 1931 .... LAUGHING SINNERS released (Johnny's role was cut from the film and he was replaced by Clark Gable).
July 1933 .... 1st serial, (FIGHTING WITH KIT CARSON) released.
September 20, 1933 .... Son, John Lachlan Brown, born.
July 1935 .... Starred in his 1st B-Western, BRANDED A COWARD.
April 4, 1939 .... Daughter, Cynthia Foster Brown, born.
May 1939 .... Last serial released (THE OREGON TRAIL).
September 1939 .... 1st movie for Universal released (DESPERATE TRAILS), also first with movie with Bob Baker.
May 1940 .... Last movie with Bob Baker released (BADMAN FROM RED BUTTE).
July 1940 .... 1st solo starring film for Universal released (SON OF ROARING DAN).
September 1942 .... 1st movie co-starring with Tex Ritter released (DEEP IN THE HEART OF TEXAS).
April 1943 .... 1st movie for Monogram released (THE GHOST RIDER).
August 1943 .... Last movie with Tex Ritter released, and the last movie for Universal (THE LONE STAR TRAIL).

September 14, 1946 .... Daughter, Sally Hester Brown born.
October 1952.................. Last starring film released (CANYON AMBUSH).
1957 .... Voted to the College Football Hall of Fame.
January 1966.................. Last big screen appearance (APACHE UPRISING).
1969 .... Inducted to the State of Alabama Sports Hall of Fame.
November 14, 1974 .... Johnny dies at the Motion Picture & TV Hospital.
November 20, 1986 .... Connie dies at the Motion Picture & TV Hospital.
July 8, 1997 .... Daughter, Jane Harriet Brown, dies
January 2000.................. Inducted into the Rose Bowl Hall of Fame.
September 21, 2003 .... First inductee to World Gun Spinning Hall of Fame.
March 13, 2004 .... Inducted into Alabama Stage & Screen Hall of Fame.
August 7, 2004 .... Honored with a Golden Boot Award.

Johnny admires his son's newly-discovered friend.

JOHNNY'S CHILDREN AND GRANDCHILDREN

Cynthia Brown married Dan Hale in 1960.
Locky Brown married Margot Chevalier in 1963.
Sally Brown Married Pal Bergan in 1970.
Jane Harriet Brown never married.

Locky & Margot's children:
Christopher Foster Brown .... born 1963
Elizabeth Walden Brown .... born 1966
Jennifer Ann Brown .... born 1969
Katherine McGilivray Brown ... born 1972

Cynthia & Dan's children:
Danny Mack Hale .... born 1965
Heather Jane Hale .... born 1967
James Ashley Hale (Ashley)... born 1968

Sally & Pal Bergan's children:
Jon Edvard Bergan.................. birth date unknown
Pal Andreas Bergan .... birth date unknown

FILMOGRAPHY

Silent Films	Year	Brown's role
Slide, Kelly, Slide	(1927)	(uncredited)
Bugle Call, The	(1927)	(uncredited)
Mockery	(1927)	Officer at table
Fair Co-Ed, The	(1927)	Bob
Divine Woman, The	(1928)	Jean Lery
Soft Living	(1928)	Stockney Webb
Square Crooks	(1928)	Larry Scott
Play Girl, The	(1928)	Bradley Lane

Sound Feature Films

(Thanks to Les Adams)

Release Date	Title	Company	Director	Sidekick	Star	Leading Lady	Brown's Role
10/14/28	OUR DANCING DAUGHTERS	M-G-M	Harry Beaumont	N/A	Joan Crawford	Joan Crawford	Ben Blaine
11/18/28	ANNAPOLIS	RKO Pathe	Christy Cabann	N/A	Johnny Mack Brown	Jeanette Loff	Bill
12/5/28	LADY OF CHANCE, A	M-G-M	Robert Z. Leonard	N/A	Norma Shearer	Norma Shearer	Steve Crandall
12/15/28	WOMAN OF AFFAIRS, A	M-G-M	Clarence Brown	N/A	Greta Garbo	Greta Garbo	David Furness
4/6/29	COQUETTE	United Artists	Sam Taylor	N/A	Mary Pickford	Mary Pickford	Michael Jeffrey
5/19/29	VALIANT, THE	Fox	William K. Howard	N/A	Paul Muni	N/A	Robert Ward
7/29/29	SINGLE STANDARD, THE	M-G-M	John Robertson	N/A	Greta Garbo	Greta Garbo	Tommy Hewlett
9/30/29	HURRICANE	Columbia	Ralph Ince	N/A	Johnny Mack Brown	Leila Hyams	Dan
11/3/29	JAZZ HEAVEN	RKO	Melville Brown	N/A	Johnny Mack Brown	Sally O'Neill	Barry Holmes
2/23/30	UNDERTOW	Universal	Harry Pollard	N/A	Johnny Mack	Mary Nolan	Paul Whalen

3/20/30	MONTANA MOON	M-G-M	Malcolm St. Clair	N/A	Joan Crawford	Joan Crawford	Larry Kerrigan
10/19/30	BILLY THE KID	M-G-M	King Vidor	N/A	Johnny Mack Brown	Kay Johnson	Billy the Kid
1/24/31	GREAT MEADOW, THE	M-G-M	Charles Brabin	N/A	Johnny Mack Brown	Eleanor Boardman	Berk Jarvis
4/25/31	SECRET SIX, THE	M-G-M	George Hill	N/A	Wallace Beery	N/A	Hank Rogers
5/30/31	LAUGHING SINNERS (aka COMPLETE SURRENDER)	M-G-M	Harry Beaumont	N/A	Joan Crawford	N/A	(Replaced by Clark Gable)
8/29/31	LAST FLIGHT, THE	Warners	William Dieterle	N/A	Richard Barthele mess	Helen Chandler	Bill Talbot
10/13/31	LASCA OF THE RIO GRANDE	Universal	Edward Laemmle	N/A	Leo Carrillo	Dorothy Burgess	Texas Ranger Miles Kincaid
5/30/32	FLAMES	Monogram	Karl Brown	N/A	Johnny Mack Brown	Noel Francis	Charlie
7/29/32	VANISHING FRONTIER, THE	Paramount	Phil Rosen	N/A	Johnny Mack Brown	Evalyn Knapp	Kirby Tornell
9/2/32	SEVENTY THOUSAND (70,000) WITNESSES	Paramount	Ralph Murphy	N/A	Philips Holmes	Dorothy Jordan	Wally Clark
11/1/32	MALAY NIGHTS (aka SHADOWS OF SINGAPORE)	Mayfair	E. Mason Hopper	N/A	Johnny Mack Brown	Dorothy Burgess	Lead Man
4/1/33	HOLLYWOOD ON PARADE No. 9	Paramount	Louis Lewyn	N/A	N/A	N/A	Himself
7/1/33	FIGHTING WITH KIT CARSON	Mascot	Armand Shaefer & Colbert Clark	Noah Beery Jr.	Johnny Mack Brown	N/A	Kit Carson
10/14/33	SATURDAY'S MILLIONS	Universal	Edward Sedgwick	N/A	Robert Young	Liela Hyams	Alan
11/4/33	FEMALE	Warners	Michael Curtiz	N/A	Ruth Chatterto n	N/A	George Cooper
12/23/33	SON OF A SAILOR	Warners	Lloyd Bacon	N/A	Joe E. Brown	Jean Muri	The Duke
4/15/34	ST. LOUIS WOMAN (aka MISSOURI NIGHTINGALE)	Mayfair	Albert Ray	N/A	Johnny Mack Brown	Jeanette Loff	Jim Warren
5/7/34	THREE ON A HONEYMOON	Fox	James Tinling	N/A	Charles Starrett	Sally Eilers	Chuck Wells

5/18/34	MARRYING WIDOWS	Tower	Sam Newfield	N/A	Minna Gombell	Judith Allen	Lead Man
7/6/34	CROSS STREETS	Chesterfield	Frank Strayer	N/A	Johnny Mack Brown	Anita Louise	Adam Blythe
9/21/34	BELLE OF THE NINETIES	Paramount	Leo McCarey	N/A	Mae West	Mae West	Brooks Claybourne
11/21/34	AGAINST THE LAW	Columbia	Lambert Hillyer	N/A	Johnny Mack Brown	Sally Blane	Steve Wayne
12/5/34	STAR NIGHT AT THE COCOANUT GROVE	Paramount	Louis Lewyn	N/A	N/A	N/A	Himself
1/15/35	RUSTLERS OF RED DOG, THE	Universal	Louis Friedlander (Lew Landers)	Raymond Hatton	Johnny Mack Brown	Joyce Compton	Jack Woods
7/1/35	BRANDED A COWARD	Supreme	Sam Newfield	Syd Saylor	Johnny Mack Brown	Billie Seward	Johnny Hume & Bill Hume
11/29/35	BETWEEN MEN	Supreme	Robert N. Bradbury	N/A	Johnny Mack Brown	Beth Marion	John Wellington Jr.
12/13/35	COURAGEOUS AVENGER, THE	Supreme	Robert N. Bradbury	N/A	Johnny Mack Brown	Helen Erickson	Kirk Baxter
1/25/36	VALLEY OF THE LAWLESS	Supreme	Robert N. Bradbury	N/A	Johnny Mack Brown	Joyce Compton	Bruce Reynolds
3/10/36	DESERT PHANTOM	Supreme	S. Roy Luby	N/A	Johnny Mack Brown	Sheila Manors(Manners)	Billy Donovan
4/25/36	ROGUE OF THE RANGE	Supreme	S. Roy Luby	N/A	Johnny Mack Brown	Lois January & Phyllis Hume	Dan Doran
6/10/36	EVERYMAN'S LAW	Supreme	Albert Ray	N/A	Johnny Mack Brown	Beth Marion	Johnny, the Dog Town Kid
7/26/36	CROOKED TRAIL, THE	Supreme	S. Roy Luby	N/A	Johnny Mack Brown	Lucile Browne	Jim Blake
9/24/36	UNDERCOVER MAN	Republic	Albert Ray	N/A	Johnny Mack Brown	Suzanne Kaaren	Steve McLain
11/23/36	LAWLESS LAND	Republic	Albert Ray	Horace Murphy	Johnny Mack Brown	Louise Stanley	Jeff Hayden
2/15/37	GAMBLING TERROR, THE	Republic	Sam Newfield	Horace Murphy	Johnny Mack Brown	Iris Meredith	Jeff Hayes
3/29/37	TRAIL OF VENGEANCE	Republic	Sam Newfield	N/A	Johnny Mack	Iris Meredith	Kenneth Early (Dude Ramsey)

4/22/37	**BAR Z BADMEN**	**Republic**	**Sam Newfield**	**N/A**	**Johnny Mack Brown**	**Lois January**	**Jim Walters**
5/13/37	**GUNS IN THE DARK**	**Republic**	**Sam Newfield**	**Syd Saylor**	**Johnny Mack Brown**	**Claire Rochelle**	**Johnny Darrell/Steve Darrow**
6/21/37	**LAWMAN IS BORN, A**	**Republic**	**Sam Newfield**	**Al St. John**	**Johnny Mack Brown**	**Iris Meredith**	**Tom Mitchell**
7/1/37	**WILD WEST DAYS**	**Universal**	**Ford Beebe & Cliff Smith**	**Frank Yaconelli & Bob Kortman**	**Johnny Mack Brown**	**Lynn Gilbert**	**Kentucky Wade**
8/2/37	**BOOTHILL BRIGADE**	**Republic**	**Sam Newfield**	**Horace Murphy**	**Johnny Mack Brown**	**Claire Rochelle**	**Lon Cardigan**
12/31/37	**WELLS FARGO**	**Paramount**	**Frank Lloyd**	**N/A**	**Joel McCrea**	**N/A**	**Talbot Carter**
4/8/38	**BORN TO THE WEST**	**Paramount**	**Charles Barton**	**N/A**	**John Wayne**	**Marsha Hunt**	**Tom Fillmore**
5/1/38	**FLAMING FRONTIERS**	**Universal**	**Alan James & Ray Taylor**	**N/A**	**Johnny Mack Brown**	**Eleanor Hansen**	**Tex Houston**
1/28/39	**SCREEN SNAPSHOTS - Star Sports**	**Columbia**	**Ralph Staub**	**N/A**	**N/A**	**N/A**	**Himself**
5/1/39	**OREGON TRAIL, THE**	**Universal**	**Ford Beebe & Saul A. Goodkind**	**Fuzzy Knight**	**Johnny Mack Brown**	**Louise Stanley**	**Jeff Scott**
9/8/39	**DESPERATE TRAILS**	**Universal**	**Albert Ray**	**Bob Baker & Fuzzy Knight**	**Johnny Mack Brown**	**Frances Robinson**	**Steve Hayden**
10/10/39	**OKLAHOMA FRONTIER**	**Universal**	**Ford Beebe**	**Bob Baker & Fuzzy Knight**	**Johnny Mack Brown**	**Anne Gwynne**	**Jeff McLeod**
11/29/39	**CHIP OF THE FLYING U**	**Universal**	**Ralph Staub**	**Bob Baker & Fuzzy Knight**	**Johnny Mack Brown**	**Doris Weston**	**Chip Bennett**
1/19/40	**WEST OF CARSON CITY**	**Universal**	**Ray Taylor**	**Bob Baker & Fuzzy Knight**	**Johnny Mack Brown**	**Peggy Moran**	**Jim Bannister**
4/5/40	**RIDERS OF PASCO BASIN**	**Universal**	**Ray Taylor**	**Bob Baker & Fuzzy Knight**	**Johnny Mack Brown**	**Frances Robinson**	**Lee Jamison**
5/31/40	**BAD MAN FROM RED BUTTE**	**Universal**	**Ray Taylor**	**Bob Baker & Fuzzy Knight**	**Johnny Mack Brown**	**Anne Gwynne**	**Buck Halliday & Gils Brady**

7/26/40	SON OF ROARING DAN	Universal	Ford Beebe	Fuzzy Knight	Johnny Mack Brown	Nell O'Day & Jeanne Kelly (Brooks)	Jim Reardon
9/20/40	RAGTIME COWBOY JOE	Universal	Ray Taylor	Fuzzy Knight	Johnny Mack Brown	Nell O'Day & Marilyn (Lynn) Merrick	Steve Stanley
11/28/40	LAW AND ORDER	Universal	Ray Taylor	Fuzzy Knight	Johnny Mack Brown	Nell O'Day	Bill Ralston
12/12/40	PONY POST	Universal	Ray Taylor	Fuzzy Knight	Johnny Mack Brown	Nell O'Day & Dorothy Short	Cal Sheridan
1/10/41	BOSS OF BULLION CITY	Universal	Ray Taylor	Fuzzy Knight	Johnny Mack Brown	Nell O'Day & Maria Montez	Tom Bryant
3/21/41	BURY ME NOT ON THE LONE PRAIRIE	Universal	Ray Taylor	Fuzzy Knight	Johnny Mack Brown	Nell O'Day & Kathryn Adams	Joe Henderson
6/20/41	LAW OF THE RANGE	Universal	Ray Taylor	Fuzzy Knight	Johnny Mack Brown	Nell O'Day & Elaine Morley	Steve Howard
7/18/41	RAWHIDE RANGERS	Universal	Ray Taylor	Fuzzy Knight	Johnny Mack Brown	Nell O'Day & Kathryn Adams	Brand Calhoun
9/5/41	MAN FROM MONTANA	Universal	Ray Taylor	Fuzzy Knight	Johnny Mack Brown	Nell O'Day & Jeanne Kelly (Brooks)	Sheriff Bob Dawson
10/17/41	SCREEN SNAPSHOTS (Series21-No.3) - 3853	Columbia	Ralph Staub	N/A	N/A	N/A	Himself
10/24/41	MASKED RIDER, THE	Universal	Ford Beebe	Fuzzy Knight	Johnny Mack Brown	Nell O'Day & Virginia Carroll	Larry Prescott
11/14/41	ARIZONA CYCLONE	Universal	Joseph H. Lewis	Fuzzy Knight	Johnny Mack Brown	Nell O'Day & Kathryn Adams	Tom Baxter
12/19/41	FIGHTING BILL FARGO	Universal	Ray Taylor	Fuzzy Knight	Johnny Mack Brown	Nell O'Day & Jeanne Kelly(Brooks)	Bill Fargo
2/13/42	RIDE 'EM COWBOY	Universal	Arthur Lubin	N/A	Abbott & Costello	Anne Gwynne	Alabama Brewster
2/13/42	STAGECOACH BUCKAROO	Universal	Ray Taylor	Fuzzy Knight	Johnny Mack Brown	Nell O'Day & Anne Nagel	Steve Hardin
8/5/42	SILVER BULLET, THE	Universal	Joseph H. Lewis	Fuzzy Knight	Johnny Mack Brown	Jennifer Holt	Silver Jim Donovan

8/21/42	BOSS OF HANGTOWN MESA	Universal	Ray Taylor	Fuzzy Knight	Johnny Mack Brown	Helen Deverall	Steve Collins
9/25/42	DEEP IN THE HEART OF TEXAS	Universal	Elmer Clifton	Tex Ritter & Fuzzy Knight	Johnny Mack Brown	Jennifer Holt	Jim Mallory
11/13/42	LITTLE JOE , THE WRANGLER	Universal	Lewis Collins	Tex Ritter & Fuzzy Knight	Johnny Mack Brown	Jennifer Holt	Neal Wallace
12/11/42	OLD CHISHOLM TRAIL, THE	Universal	Elmer Clifton	Tex Ritter & Fuzzy Knight	Johnny Mack Brown	Jennifer Holt	Dusty Gardner
2/5/43	TENTING TONIGHT ON THE OLD CAMP GROUND	Universal	Lewis Collins	Tex Ritter & Fuzzy Knight	Johnny Mack Brown	Jennifer Holt	Wade Benson
4/2/43	GHOST RIDER, THE	Monogram	Wallace W. Fox	Raymond Hatton	Johnny Mack Brown	Beverly Boyd	Nevada Jack McKenzie
4/29/43	CHEYENNE ROUNDUP	Universal	Ray Taylor	Tex Ritter & Fuzzy Knight	Johnny Mack Brown	Jennifer Holt	Buck Brandon & Gils Brandon
6/4/43	RAIDERS OF SAN JOAQUIN	Universal	Lewis Collins	Tex Ritter & Fuzzy Knight	Johnny Mack Brown	Jennifer Holt	Rocky Morgan
7/16/43	STRANGER FROM PECOS, THE	Monogram	Lambert Hillyer	Raymond Hatton	Johnny Mack Brown	Christine McIntyre	Nevada Jack McKenzie
8/6/43	LONE STAR TRAIL, THE	Universal	Ray Taylor	Tex Ritter & Fuzzy Knight	Johnny Mack Brown	Jennifer Holt	Blaze Barker
9/3/43	SIX GUN GOSPEL	Monogram	Lambert Hillyer	Raymond Hatton	Johnny Mack Brown	Inna Gest	Nevada Jack McKenzie
10/15/43	OUTLAWS OF STAMPEDE PASS	Monogram	Wallace W. Fox	Raymond Hatton	Johnny Mack Brown	Ellen Hall	Nevada Jack McKenzie
11/26/43	TEXAS KID, THE	Monogram	Lambert Hillyer	Raymond Hatton	Johnny Mack Brown	Shirley Patterson	Nevada Jack McKenzie
1/31/44	RAIDERS OF THE BORDER	Monogram	John P. McCarthy	Raymond Hatton	Johnny Mack Brown	Ellen Hall	Nevada Jack McKenzie
3/28/44	PARTNERS OF THE TRAIL	Monogram	Lambert Hillyer	Raymond Hatton	Johnny Mack Brown	Christine McIntyre	Nevada Jack McKenzie
4/25/44	LAW MEN	Monogram	Lambert Hillyer	Raymond Hatton	Johnny Mack Brown	Jan Wiley	Nevada Jack McKenzie
6/24/44	RANGE LAW	Monogram	Lambert Hillyer	Raymond Hatton	Johnny Mack Brown	Ellen Hall	Nevada Jack McKenzie

8/5/44	WEST OF THE RIO GRANDE	Monogram	Lambert Hillyer	Raymond Hatton	Johnny Mack Brown	Christine McIntyre	Nevada Jack McKenzie
9/16/44	LAND OF THE OUTLAWS	Monogram	Lambert Hillyer	Raymond Hatton	Johnny Mack Brown	Nan Holliday	Nevada Jack McKenzie
11/4/44	LAW OF THE VALLEY	Monogram	Howard Bretherton	Raymond Hatton	Johnny Mack Brown	Lynne Carver	Nevada Jack McKenzie
11/17/44	GHOST GUNS	Monogram	Lambert Hillyer	Raymond Hatton	Johnny Mack Brown	Evelyn Finley	Nevada Jack McKenzie
1/15/45	NAVAJO TRAIL, THE	Monogram	Howard Bretherton	Raymond Hatton	Johnny Mack Brown	Jennifer Holt	Nevada Jack McKenzie
2/2/45	FOREVER YOURS	Monogram	William Nigh	N/A	Gale Storm	Gale Storm	Major Tex O'Connor
2/16/45	GUN SMOKE	Monogram	Howard Bretherton	Raymond Hatton	Johnny Mack Brown	Jennifer Holt	Nevada Jack McKenzie
5/15/45	STRANGER FROM SANTA FE	Monogram	Lambert Hillyer	Raymond Hatton	Johnny Mack Brown	Beatrive Gray & Joann Curtis	Nevada Jack McKenzie
6/25/45	FLAME OF THE WEST	Monogram	Lambert Hillyer	Raymond Hatton	Johnny Mack Brown	Joan Woodbury	Dr. John Poole
10/20/45	LOST TRAIL, THE	Monogram	Lambert Hillyer	Raymond Hatton	Johnny Mack Brown	Jennifer Holt	Nevada Jack McKenzie
11/25/45	FRONTIER FEUD	Monogram	Lambert Hillyer	Raymond Hatton	Johnny Mack Brown	Christine McIntyre	Nevada Jack McKenzie
1/2/46	BORDER BANDITS	Monogram	Lambert Hillyer	Raymond Hatton	Johnny Mack Brown	Rosa Del Rosario	Nevada Jack McKenzie
1/26/46	DRIFTING ALONG	Monogram	Derwin Abrahams	Raymond Hatton	Johnny Mack Brown	Lynne Carver	Steve Garner
3/2/46	HAUNTED MINE , THE	Monogram	Derwin Abrahams	Raymond Hatton	Johnny Mack Brown	Linda Johnson (Melinda Leighton)	Nevada Jack McKenzie
5/27/46	UNDER ARIZONA SKIES	Monogram	Lambert Hillyer	Raymond Hatton	Johnny Mack Brown	Reno Blair (Brown)	Dusty Smith
6/8/46	GENTLEMAN FROM TEXAS , THE	Monogram	Lambert Hillyer	Raymond Hatton	Johnny Mack Brown	Claudia Drake, Reno Blair & Christine McIntyre	Johnny Macklin

6/10/46	SCREEN SNAPSHOTS (7860) -Famous Fathers and Sons	Columbia	Ralph Staub	N/A	N/A	N/A	Himself
9/21/46	TRIGGER FINGERS	Monogram	Lambert Hillyer	Raymond Hatton	Johnny Mack Brown	Jennifer Holt	Sam "Hurricane" Benton
10/16/46	SHADOWS ON THE RANGE	Monogram	Lambert Hillyer	Raymond Hatton	Johnny Mack Brown	Jan Bryant	John Mason
11/16/46	SILVER RANGE	Monogram	Lambert Hillyer	Raymond Hatton	Johnny Mack Brown	Jan Bryant	Johnny Bronton
1/18/47	RAIDERS OF THE SOUTH	Monogram	Lambert Hillyer	Raymond Hatton	Johnny Mack Brown	Evelyn Brent & Reno Blair	Captain Johnny Brownell
2/15/47	VALLEY OF FEAR	Monogram	Lambert Hillyer	Raymond Hatton	Johnny Mack Brown	Christine McIntyre	Johnny Williams
3/29/47	TRAILING DANGER	Monogram	Lambert Hillyer	Raymond Hatton	Johnny Mack Brown	Peggy Wynne	Johnny
4/26/47	LAND OF THE LAWLESS	Monogram	Lambert Hillyer	Raymond Hatton	Johnny Mack Brown	Christine McIntyre & June Harrison	Johnny Mack
5/24/47	LAW COMES TO GUNSIGHT, THE	Monogram	Lambert Hillyer	Raymond Hatton	Johnny Mack Brown	Reno Blair (Brown)	Johnny Macklin
6/28/47	CODE OF THE SADDLE	Monogram	Thomas Carr	Raymond Hatton	Johnny Mack Brown	Kay Morley	Johnny Macklin
7/16/47	FLASHING GUNS	Monogram	Lambert Hillyer	Raymond Hatton	Johnny Mack Brown	Jan Bryant	Johnny Mack
9/4/47	SCREEN SNAPSHOTS (9851)- Hollywood Cowboys	Columbia	Ralph Staub	N/A	N/A	N/A	Himself
10/25/47	PRAIRIE EXPRESS	Monogram	Lambert Hillyer	Raymond Hatton	Johnny Mack Brown	Virginia Belmont	Johnny Hudson
12/20/47	GUN TALK	Monogram	Lambert Hillyer	Raymond Hatton	Johnny Mack Brown	Christine McIntyre & Geneva Gray	Johnny McVey
4/11/48	CROSSED TRAILS	Monogram	Lambert Hillyer	Raymond Hatton	Johnny Mack Brown	Lynne Carver	Johnny Mack
5/16/48	FRONTIER AGENT	Monogram	Lambert Hillyer	Raymond Hatton	Johnny Mack Brown	Reno Blair (Brown)	Johnny Mack Brown

6/20/48	TRIGGERMAN	Monogram	Howard Bretherton	Raymond Hatton	Johnny Mack Brown	Virginia Carroll	Johnny Mack Brown
7/18/48	BACK TRAIL	Monogram	Christy Cabanne	Raymond Hatton	Johnny Mack Brown	Mildred Coles	Johnny Mack Brown
8/15/48	FIGHTING RANGER, THE	Monogram	Lewis Collins	Raymond Hatton	Johnny Mack Brown	Christine Larson	Johnny Mack
10/3/48	SHERIFF OF MEDICINE BOW, THE	Monogram	Lambert Hillyer	Max Terhune & Raymond Hatton	Johnny Mack Brown	Evelyn Finley	Sheriff John Mack Brown
11/7/48	GUNNING FOR JUSTICE	Monogram	Ray Taylor	Max Terhune & Raymond Hatton	Johnny Mack Brown	Evelyn Finley	Johnny Mack
12/12/48	HIDDEN DANGER	Monogram	Ray Taylor	Max Terhune & Raymond Hatton	Johnny Mack Brown	Christine Larson	Johnny Mack
1/31/49	OVERLAND TRAILS	Monogram	Lambert Hillyer	Raymond Hatton	Johnny Mack Brown	Virginia Belmont	Johnny Murdock
2/20/49	LAW OF THE WEST	Monogram	Ray Taylor	Max Terhune	Johnny Mack Brown	Gerry Patterson	Johnny Mack
4/3/49	TRAIL'S END	Monogram	Lambert Hillyer	Max Terhune	Johnny Mack Brown	Kay Morley	Johnny Mack
5/1/49	STAMPEDE	Allied Artist	Lesley Selander	N/A	Rod Cameron	N/A	Sheriff Aaron Ball
6/5/49	WEST OF ELDORADO	Monogram	Ray Taylor	Max Terhune	Johnny Mack Brown	Reno Brown	Johnny Mack
7/16/49	RANGE JUSTICE	Monogram	Ray Taylor	Max Terhune	Johnny Mack Brown	Felice Ingersall	Johnny Mack Brown
10/9/49	WESTERN RENEGADES	Monogram	Wallace W. Fox	Max Terhune	Johnny Mack Brown	Jane Adams	Marshal Johnny Mack Brown
2/19/50	WEST OF WYOMING	Monogram	Wallace W. Fox	Milburn Morante	Johnny Mack Brown	Gail Davis	Johnny Mack Brown
3/12/50	OVER THE BORDER	Monogram	Wallace W. Fox	Milburn Morante	Johnny Mack Brown	Wendy Waldron	Johnny Mack Brown
4/30/50	SIX GUN MESA	Monogrm	Wallace W. Fox	Milburn Morante	Johnny Mack Brown	Gail Davis	Johnny Mack Brown

9/17/50	LAW OF THE PANHANDLE	Monogram	Lewis Collins	Milburn Morante	Johnny Mack Brown	Jane Adams	Johnny Mack
11/26/50	OUTLAW GOLD	Monogram	Wallace W. Fox	Milburn Morante	Johnny Mack Brown	Jane Adams	Dave Willis
12/24/50	SHORT GRASS	Allied Artist	Lesley Selander	N/A	Rod Cameron	N/A	Sheriff Keown
1/14/51	COLORADO AMBUSH	Monogram	Lewis Collins	N/A	Johnny Mack Brown	Lois Hall	Johnny Mack Brown
3/11/51	MAN FROM SONORA	Monogram	Lewis Collins	House Peters Jr.	Johnny Mack Brown	Phyllis Coates	Johnny Mack Brown
5/6/51	BLAZING BULLETS	Monogram	Wallace W. Fox	House Peters Jr.	Johnny Mack Brown	Lois Hall	Johnny Mack Brown
7/24/51	MONTANA DESPERADO	Monogram	Wallace W. Fox	N/A	Johnny Mack Brown	Virginia Herrick	Dave Borden
8/19/51	OKLAHOMA JUSTICE	Monogram	Lewis Collins	Jimmy Ellison	Johnny Mack Brown	Phyllis Coates	Johnny Mack Brown
10/7/51	WHISTLING HILLS	Monogram	Derwin Abrahams	Jimmy Ellison	Johnny Mack Brown	Noel Neill	Johnny Mack Brown
12/2/51	TEXAS LAWMEN	Monogram	Lewis Collins	Jimmy Ellison	Johnny Mack Brown	None	Johnny Mack Brown
1/27/52	TEXAS CITY	Monogram	Lewis Collins	Jimmy Ellison	Johnny Mack Brown	Lois Hall	Johnny Mack Brown
3/20/52	MAN FROM THE BLACK HILLS	Monogram	Thomas Carr	Jimmy Ellison	Johnny Mack Brown	None	Johnny Mack Brown
7/20/52	DEAD MAN'S TRAIL	Monogram	Lewis Collins	Jimmy Ellison	Johnny Mack Brown	Barbara Allen	Johnny Mack Brown
10/12/52	CANYON AMBUSH	Monogram	Lewis Collins	Lee Roberts	Johnny Mack Brown	Phyllis Coates	Johnny Mack Brown
4/26/53	SCREEN SNAPSHOTS (5860) - Out West in Hollywood	Columbia	Ralph Staub	N/A	N/A	N/A	Himself
6/26/53	MARSHAL'S DAUGHTER, THE	United Artists	William Berke	N/A	Laurie Anders & Hoot Gibson	N/A	Himself
6/30/65	REQUIEM FOR A GUNFIGHTER	Embassy	Spencer G. Bennet	N/A	Rod Cameron	N/A	Enkoff
7/31/65	BOUNTY KILLER, THE	Embassy	Spencer G. Bennet	N/A	Dan Duryea	N/A	Sheriff Green

1/15/66	APACHE UPRISING	Paramount	R.G. Springsteen	N/A	Rory Calhoun	N/A	Sheriff Ben Hall

Les Adams added some tidbits and footnotes: Of the total of 131 westerns and western serials Brown was in, Lambert Hillyer and Ray Taylor directed 52 of them. Of the total of 131 westerns and western serials Brown was in, Raymond Hatton (46) and Fuzzy Knight (29) were his sidekicks in 75 of them. He also was in other films with both of them, but this number is for their Brown-sidekick roles.

This list is in order of release and not production order, so some of the finished Universal films were released after he went to Monogram. This isn't the only instance where a B-Western star changed studios, and his new films were competing against his other series.

Johnny also made a comedy short with Raymond Hatton in 1931 called Hollywood Halfbacks.

Occasionally, Johhnny picked up a little extra money with endorsements.

ESSENTIAL VIEWING OF JOHNNY'S WESTERNS

The following reviews were written by Boyd Magers, publisher of *Western Clippings* (highly recommended), 1312 Stagecoach Road SE, Albuquerque, New Mexico 87123, (505) 292-0049. Magers is also the author of several books and a recognized authority on Western films and performers.

(Author's Note: This is only a partial listing of recommended movies and doesn't mean that Johnny did not make more outstanding Westerns.)

BRANDED A COWARD (1935 Supreme)
After witnessing his parent's deaths at the hands of a notorious outlaw, the Cat, as well as being separated from his brother by the outlaws, Johnny Mack Brown grows up hiding his fear of guns and violence. He regains himself when he rescues Billie Seward from stagecoach bandits and is made town marshal only to find the Cat is the outlaw terrorizing the region — but surprise, this is a new Cat. But that's not the end of the surprises in this superior B-Western. Not to be missed. Mickey Rentschler and Rex Downing play Brown and his brother at a younger age. Yakima Canutt, doubling for Brown, performs his fall from the six-up, under the stage, grab-the-back-end stunt. Remade in 1950 as FAST ON THE DRAW with Jimmy Ellison and Russell Hayden.

BETWEEN MEN (1935 Supreme)
The second entry in Johnny Mack Brown's series for producer A. W. Hackel is a perfect example of how an intelligent script (Charles Francis Royal), good acting (strong performance by William Farnum in a role almost equal to Brown's) and thoughtful directing (Robert North Bradbury) can elevate a B-Western far beyond its norm. Certainly, coincidence is the name of the game in Royal's story as Virginia blacksmith Farnum flees west, mistakenly believing he is responsible for the death of his young son. Actually, the boy was only hurt in the melee and is adopted by wealthy Lloyd Ingraham who, two decades later, sends the now grown Brown to New Mexico to locate his granddaughter, Beth Marion, the child of the daughter Ingraham disowned for marrying rancher Frank Ball. In New Mexico, Ball is having trouble keeping slimy ranch hand Earl Dwire away from pretty Beth. Dwire works for Farnum, who has assumed a new name and identity. To get even, Dwire and his rustlers (Sherry Tansey, Budd Buster) steal Ball's cattle and kidnap Beth. Ball is killed but Brown and new found prospector friend Milburn Morante rescue Beth.

Farnum swears to get Dwire for Ball's killing and hires Brown to help him, not realizing, of course, Brown is his son. Protective of Ball's daughter (Beth), and mistakenly thinking Brown has seduced her, Farnum engages Brown in a fight at a remote cabin (reminding older viewers of Farnum's classic battle with Tom Santschi in THE SPOILERS ('14). During the fracas Farnum sees a birthmark on Brown and realizes he is his son. But — there's still Dwire's gang to contend with. It's a complicated plot, but director Bradbury moves it along at a steady pace, wringing out every moment of drama possible. In the ranks of B-Westerns, this is an important picture. It's worth noting, perennial B-Western player Budd Buster plays two roles, as a Virginia townsperson, then as one of Dwire's rustlers.

VALLEY OF THE LAWLESS (1936 Supreme)
Johnny Mack Brown tracks down outlaw George Hayes to locate a treasure map Hayes stole from Brown's parents years ago. Forced to flee, he never dug up the treasure but has the map to the buried gold tattooed on his chest. Two former members of Hayes' gang come after him and he is mortally wounded. Before he dies he reveals the map to his grandkids, Joyce Compton and Bobby Nelson, who, with their father, Frank Ball, head for the Valley of the Lawless where the gold is buried. The Valley is controlled by renegade Frank Hagney and his gunmen (Charlie King, Blackie Whiteford). Meanwhile, Sheriff Jack Rockwell sends his son Dennis Meadows (later Moore) to scout the valley. Dennis has always been in love with Compton, but Compton has fallen for Johnny Mack after he protected them from Hagney's gang. Charles Francis Royal's plot gets even more involved, with exciting new developments every five minutes. Not a frame is wasted in Robert North Bradbury's direction making this another supreme Supreme. Cowboy cancer alert: Brown smokes (to make him appear tougher, like an outlaw).

THE CROOKED TRAIL (1936 Supreme)
Most of Johnny Mack Brown's Supreme titles were a bit more adult in approach and story content and this tale of murder, love and reformation is no exception as Brown befriends killer John Merton in his gold mining claim. But both of them need to watch out for that double-crossing snake in black, gambler Charlie King, who is engaged to Lucile Browne although she ends up marrying Johnny Mack midway when King is exposed as a crook. With fine direction by S. Roy Luby (1899-1976) and a taut script by George Plympton, CROOKED TRAIL proves what could be accomplished within the confines of a B-Western. Truly, A-western material in the 60 minute B-Western format. Rare chance to see veteran heavy Dick Curtis on the right side of the law as a miner.

THE GAMBLING TERROR (1937 Supreme)
A town is besieged by Charlie King's ruthless desperadoes (Dick Curtis, Frank Ellis, Sherry Tansey) demanding protection money. Despite the efforts of courageous newspaper editor Frank Ball and his daughter, gorgeous Iris Meredith, it seems as if the gang, with a mystery man leader, cannot be stopped. Enter Johnny Mack Brown, a tough, no-nonsense gambler, who will not be intimidated by the ruffians. Eventually, the gang holds Bobby Nelson (Iris' young brother) prisoner, which brings about their downfall. The mystery boss angle is better handled here than in any B-Western I've ever seen. Your choices are stableman Budd Buster, lawyer Earl Dwire, Sheriff Ted Adams, bartender Steve Clark and goofy, drunkard printer Horace Murphy. This one's of more than passing interest with a solid script by George Plympton and Fred Myton; directed by Sam Newfield.

BORN TO THE WEST (re-released as HELL TOWN) (1937 Paramount)
Superior western entertainment. Good script, good actors, good direction (by Charles Barton) lift this Zane Grey entry into near A territory. Drifter John Wayne straightens out his slightly wayward life and woos Marsha Hunt when he becomes trail boss for cousin Johnny Mack Brown, who has to rescue Wayne before it's all over. Alan Ladd is listed in a bit role, but I defy you to spot him. Full of stock footage from earlier silent and talkie Paramount Greys. Watch for Russell Hayden, Buster Crabbe and Jack Holt (who starred in the original 1926 film, HELLTOWN) in the stock.

CHIP OF THE FLYING U (1939 Universal)
It's war on the range as 5th Columnists hide munitions on Forrest Taylor's Flying U Ranch until time to ship them by boat from the nearby cove. Johnny Mack Brown is Taylor's foreman in love with Taylor's sister, Doris Weston. Neighboring rancher Anthony Warde wants the Flying U because of its proximity to the cove, making it easier for him to supply stolen munitions to the Nazis. Knowing the loss of money might prevent Taylor from getting a loan and persuade him to sell, Warde's men (Karl Hackett and Chuck Morrison) rob the bank, killing banker Henry Hall and trying to lay blame on Brown. In his 3rd of six outings with Brown, Bob Baker is relegated to the role of back-up cowboy. He sings two songs including "Mr. Moon" (which was also sung by Frances Langford in Universal's COWBOY IN MANHATTAN ['43]) and that's about all he does. The Texas Rangers also chime-in with two and sidekick Fuzzy Knight cackles one. Based on B. M. Bower's novel, CHIP OF THE FLYING U had three previous outings ... the first with Tom Mix in '14, the second, renamed GALLOPING DUDE in '20 with Bud Osborne, and the third with Hoot Gibson in '26. For his 3rd Universal western, Brown traded in his white horse for Rebel, a palomino he'd ride for the rest of his Universal and Monogram westerns.

LAW AND ORDER (1940 Universal)
It's no holds barred as newly appointed U.S. Marshal Johnny Mack Brown brings gun law justice to Rhyolite with the help of hard riding Nell O'Day, Fuzzy Knight and gambler James Craig. They're up against the mean, tough Harry Cording, Ted Adams, Ethan Laidlaw and their gang. One of the absolute best of Brown's Universal series — if not the best. W. R. Burnett's novel, Saint Johnson, loosely based on the Earp-Clanton Tombstone, Arizona saga, was used as the basis for this film as it had been for Walter Huston's 1932 LAW AND ORDER. It was revived again for Brown's '37 serial, WILD WEST DAYS, and again for Ronald Reagan in LAW AND ORDER ('53). This was future 3 Mesquiteers member Jimmy Dodd's first exposure to film and he appears overwhelmed by it all in dialogue scenes but very comfortable singing a duet with Nell. The smooth singing Notables contribute one song. I'm sure they were fine in supper clubs but were just not right for the western milieu.

BADMAN FROM RED BUTTE (1940 Universal)
Two Johnny Mack Browns for the price of one. Twin brothers — one good, one bad. The problem arises when the town believes the good Brown is the outlaw Brown. When the outlaw Brown is killed by the town gang (Norman Willis, Earle Hodgins, Roy Barcroft) the good Brown helps elect his singing lawyer pal, Bob Baker, justice of the peace as they bring gun law and fisticuff order to the town. Anne Gwynne's the girl and Texas Jim Lewis (1909-1990) and his Lone Star Cowboys provide some music. This was Lewis' second film after appearing in CAROLINA MOON with Gene Autry. He and his group went on to

make three with Charles Starrett. Lewis made his home in Seattle after 1950, hosting SAFETY JUNCTION, a popular children's TV show. His "Squaws Along the Yukon" in '44 was later a big hit for Hank Thompson in '58.

WEST OF CARSON CITY (1940 Universal)
Gold is discovered near the ghost town of Ridgeville! That's when the lawless element run by Harry Woods and his gun-rannies (Frank Mitchell, Roy Barcroft, Charlie King, Jack Roper) take over. When even Judge Robert Homans and his daughter Peggy Moran are threatened, in steps Circle X ranch owner Johnny Mack Brown and his hands (Bob Baker, Fuzzy Knight, even Ted Wells in a small role) to strike back at the badmen. Baker, in a very secondary role, sings two songs, both of which, "On the Trail of Tomorrow" and "Let's Go", were reused a year later in ARIZONA CYCLONE by the Notables, who sing here with Baker. Thankfully, Fuzzy does not sing in this one! This is one of the few B-Westerns that can claim all three top screen badmen — Woods, Barcroft and King.

RIDERS OF PASCO BASIN (1940 Universal)
Rodeo rider Johnny Mack Brown returns to Pasco Basin to help his father-figure, newspaper editor William Gould, who is waging a campaign against crooked land promoters Arthur Loft and James Guilfoyle (and their head gunman, Ted Adams) who are promoting a phony irrigation project. Brown is helped by ranch hand Bob Baker who is in love with Brown's old girlfriend, Frances Robinson. (At one point Baker goes on a tirade about being second best to Johnny Mack's character that sounds as if he really means it. It's fairly well known Baker resented losing his own series and playing second fiddle to Brown.) When Gould is killed, leaving his young son Robert Winkler an orphan, Brown forms a vigilante group, causing a rift between he and Baker. To stir up resentment against Brown, the swindlers shoot Frank LaRue (Robinson's father) and make some other violent acts seem the work of Brown's vigilantes. Baker sings one and a half songs this outing while Rudy Sooter's Californians do one. Blessedly, Fuzzy Knight keeps his mouth shut — song wise anyhow. Fast moving hour.

ARIZONA CYCLONE (1941 Universal)
Innovative and unusual camera setups from director 'wagon wheel' Joseph H. Lewis make this a visually exciting and above average Johnny Mack Brown B-Western. Lewis also manages to rein in Fuzzy Knight's unfunny antics. Good song by the Notables — "On the Trail of Tomorrow". Neat left side of the horse mount by Johnny Mack. Good hard riding sequence with Nell O' Day at Iverson's. For talented Kathryn Adams, it's the best role among her three Browns. Wish Universal had utilized her more. When the long over-due barroom bust up between Brown and heavy Dick Curtis finally arrives, it's a doozy. This is Universal Johnny Mack Brown at its best!

THE SILVER BULLET (1942 Universal)
Silver Jim (Johnny Mack Brown) searches the west for a gunman with a lightning bolt scar on his left arm that shot him in the back with a silver bullet and murdered his father five years ago. That man is crooked incumbent Senator LeRoy Mason who, with partner Rex Lease, is embezzling money from local ranchers such as Jennifer Holt. Mason goes to Doc William Farnum to have the incriminating scar removed but when Doc gets wise, Mason kills him. Suspecting, Brown and the others stage an election rally and run Doc's widow (Claire Whitney) for Senator opposing Mason. It all winds up in a six gun show-

down as Johnny Mack 'returns' the Silver Bullet to Mason. Terrific saloon brawl and other action sequences expertly directed with his customary flair for unusual and unique camera set ups by Joseph H. Lewis. The song, "Sweetheart of the Rio Grande" (written by Oliver Drake, Jimmy Wakely and Milt Rosen), sung by Nora Lou Martin (with as sweet and pure a voice as you ever heard) and the Pals of the Golden West is worth the price of admission. You'll find yourself rewinding the tape and playing it over and over.

DEEP IN THE HEART OF TEXAS (1942 Universal)
"With the close of the Civil War, Texas, having supported the Confederacy, was refused permission to rejoin the Union until the holders of large land grants relinquished their titles and vowed new oath of allegiance. Many unscrupulous land owners refused to accept this decision and, banding together, organized the Republic of the Rio Grande, an independent territory whose boundary lines spread like wildfire across the state." Johnny Mack Brown returns from the Civil War to his home in Texas to find his father, William Farnum (in an excellent role that he makes the absolute most of), has set himself up as the ruler of the Republic of Texas and is leading a bunch of land grabbers (enforcer Harry Woods—hamming it up too much with comedy relief Fuzzy Knight—Kenneth Harlan, Ed Cobb, Earle Hodgins). They rule the Republic by force of arms. When Brown learns of this from newspaper editor Pat O'Malley and his daughter Jennifer Holt, he opposes his father to put Texas back in the Union. Tex Ritter, in his first of seven excellent features with Brown, is the representative from the Governor's office, also opposing Farnum's illegal Republic. Tex sings "Streets of Laredo", the Jimmy Wakely Trio sings one while Fuzzy gets to sing two, including the title tune. One of Universal's more ambitious and best B-Westerns.

RAIDERS OF SAN JOAQUIN (1943 Universal)
This Johnny Mack Brown/Tex Ritter co-starrer (they were now being billed as the west's greatest star team), produced by Oliver Drake and directed by Lewis Collins, gets everything right and comes out a winner. Plenty of action, lots of hard riding, well developed conflict between the two leads, a little well placed comedy from Fuzzy Knight, some music by the Jimmy Wakely Trio — all in the right amounts and format. Crooked George Eldredge-along with dry-goods store owner Henry Roquemore and dirty work henchie Jack Ingram-are trying to grab up all the ranches in the valley and blame their underhandedness on the A&M Railroad. After Eldredge has the property, he'll sell the land at a profit to an Eastern syndicate for railroad right-of-way. Opposing Eldredge, Tex Ritter's father (Joseph Bernard) is killed by gunman Carl Sepulveda. Tex exacts revenge as he and his boys become fugitives opposing Eldredge's actions, doing their best to help the lone rancher hold-out, Henry Hall and his daughter Jennifer Holt. Enter Johnny Mack Brown, actually the son of railroad owner John Elliott, who aids their fight as a mysterious Black Rider. However, in doing so, to gain Eldredge's trust in order to trap him, he alienates Ritter and Holt. Fuzzy Knight rides along with Brown but is nowhere near as obtrusive as usual. Ritter sings only one song while the Jimmy Wakely Trio get to perform two.

LONE STAR TRAIL (1943 Universal)
Framed for a robbery he didn't commit and now pardoned from prison after serving two long years, Johnny Mack Brown returns to Dead Falls to prove his innocence and rout out the men who framed him — Mayor Earle Hodgins, saloon owner Robert Mitchum and businessman Michael Vallon. Johnny is helped by new friend Tex Ritter and old pals Fuzzy

Knight (who, thankfully, does not sing in this one), Jennifer Holt, the Jimmy Wakely Trio and, supposedly, George Eldredge who is secretly the man behind the three who framed Brown. Also what no one knows except Sheriff Harry Strang is that Ritter is an undercover U.S. Marshal searching for $75,000 in unrecovered stagecoach loot. Good, solid Oliver Drake (based on a story by Victor Halperin) script and plenty of slam-bang action including a humdinger of a barroom brawl with Mitchum, Eddie Parker and Jack Ingram. This being the final pairing (they made 7 together) of Brown and Ritter, the series winds up with a real winner. Even while this film was in release, Johnny rode over to Monogram as a replacement for Buck Jones' Rough Riders series. Ritter stayed on at Universal for a few, and then wound up at PRC with Dave O'Brien. Old time stars Bob Reeves and William Desmond have bit parts in LONE STAR TRAIL.

CHEYENNE ROUNDUP (1943 Universal)
Sheriff Tex Ritter runs outlaws Gils Brandon (Johnny Mack Brown), Harry Woods, Roy Barcroft and Robert Barron out of the country. The men ride to the ghost town of El Dorado where they bamboozle Fuzzy Knight into selling them 51% of the town where Fuz's pal Budd Buster has just discovered gold. The gold rush is on; the gang takes over and runs El Dorado to their satisfaction. Vigilantes, seeking to curb the lawlessness, hire Tex Ritter as town marshal. On the day Gils' fiancée, Jennifer Holt, is due to arrive, Ritter shoots it out with the badman who escapes wounding only to die in the arms of his twin brother Buck (Johnny Mack Brown in a dual role) who has been searching the west for his twin. Dying, Gils regrets his outlawry and asks brother Buck to clean up the town. Working together, he and Ritter bring the badmen to justice. The film is a loose remake of BAD MAN FROM RED BUTTE ('40) also with Brown in a dual role. The Jimmy Wakely Trio sings two songs, Tex Ritter sings "Rose of the Hills" and Fuzzy Knight reprises "Ain't Got Nothin' and Nothin' Worries Me" from BOSS OF HANGTOWN MESA ('42). Producer Oliver Drake "borrowed" the script and remade it as LONESOME TRAIL with Jimmy Wakely in 1945 at Monogram. Director Ray Taylor's credits are extensive and he specialized in serials, some 47 or them from '28-'46 at, chiefly, Universal, but a few at Republic, Principal and Columbia. Some of the best are GORDON OF GHOST CITY ('33), VIGILANTES ARE COMING ('36), DICK TRACY ('37), SPIDER'S WEB ('38), GREEN HORNET ('39), RIDERS OF DEATH VALLEY ('41), MASTER KEY ('45), and SCARLET HORSEMAN ('46). Born in 1888, Taylor started as a stage manager, and then became an assistant director for John Ford during the silent era. His first directorial job was on Ted Wells' BORDER WILDCAT ('29 Universal). Over the years he helmed westerns with Buck Jones, 3 Mesquiteers, Tex Ritter, Johnny Mack Brown, Lash LaRue, Eddie Dean and Whip Wilson. He died in 1952.

SIX GUN GOSPEL (1943 Monogram)
By the numbers, railroad coming to town land grab, undercover stranger in town-plot, but here the 'numbers' are fast moving and well done with Johnny Mack Brown as Nevada Jack McKenzie and his sidekick Raymond Hatton battling badmen Kenneth MacDonald, Roy Barcroft (just a couple of months away from signing a long running exclusive Republic contract), Edmund Cobb and Bud Osborne. Directed by Brown regular Lambert Hillyer. One of the bright spots is Raymond Hatton, masquerading as a parson, singing "that dirty little coward that shot Mr. Howard" at the church social. Former Universal and Republic minor star Eddie Dew is wasted in the thankless part of a Wells Fargo express agent.

THE TEXAS KID (1943 Monogram)
A real showcase for Marshall Reed. And one of the best of Johnny Mack Brown's Nevada Jack MacKenzie Monogram series which had begun earlier in '43. (This was the 5th film.) It's an intricate but original screenplay from Jess Bowers (Adele Buffington) filled with crosses and double-crosses. Reed is a friend of Brown's who's also a member of Ed Cobb's hold-up gang, but is trying to go straight by buying a half interest in the trading post Shirley Patterson has sold to Robert Fiske. Unbeknownst to Reed, Fiske is the real boss behind Cobb's buzzards (Stanley Price, Lynton Brent, Charlie King [killed early on], Kermit Maynard, Bud Osborne). U.S. Marshals Brown and Raymond Hatton (posing as a peddler) round up the gang.

FLAME OF THE WEST (1945 Monogram)
Many critics rate this as one of Johnny Mack Brown's best B-Westerns. Perhaps it is, but not because of Brown who plays the mild new medical doctor in town who's sworn off guns, but rather because of the plot—dissimilar to Brown's normal Monograms—and in particular, the excellent performance by that fine actor Douglass Dumbrille as a tough town tamer sent for by the Trail Forks Citizens' Committee. Dumbrille totally steals the picture from everyone! The film is also given extra length (it runs 70 minutes) to develop its distinct plot. Trail Forks is overrun by crooked gamblers and outlaws headed up by saloon owner Harry Woods, gambler Jack Ingram and gunmen Ray Bennett, Bob Duncan and Frank McCarroll. Woods' dance hall queen is Joan Woodbury who, as we soon see, has a "history" with Dumbrille. Naturally, when Dumbrille is gunned down by the gang, Brown must reluctantly strap on his six guns to avenge his new found friend's murder. But other than that, and until then, Dumbrille owns every scene he's in. The complacent, mild tempered Brown is simply no acting match for Dumbrille's talent. Brown regular Raymond Hatton is featured, but in a totally minor role this time. Woodbury sings one song; Pee Wee King and His Golden West Cowboys do a couple (but have no speaking parts) and Johnny Mack is allowed to perform some quick gun tricks early.

HAUNTED MINE (1946 Monogram)
Murder in an old mine, a throat slashing crazed 'ghost' with a straight razor (Ray Bennett), secret passageways—Nevada Jack MacKenzie (Johnny Mack Brown) and Sandy Hopkins (Raymond Hatton) investigate and save the day for Linda Johnson and her Mom from unscrupulous John Merton and his boys (Marshall Reed, Terry Frost). Nicely paced by Derwin Abrahams. A memorable Brown that stands out from the pack.

TRAILING DANGER (1947 Monogram)
Screenwriter J. Benton Cheney turned in a nice "original" here. Outlaw leader Marshall Reed has someone in town (I. Stanford Jolley) tipping him off as to when gold shipments are going out by stagecoach. Reed is captured, and then escapes vowing vengeance on express officer Steve Darrell who set up the trap to capture him. Darrell is now riding on a cross-country stage-run which sets the "stage" for one of the most hard-riding, action-packed Johnny Mack Brown adventures as he, Darrell, and grizzled Raymond Hatton outsmart, outgun and whittle down Reed's gang (Ray Jones, Wally West, Eddie Parker, Bud Osborne, Willard Willingham) one by one. Also on the exciting stagecoach ride are Darrell's niece Peggy Wynne, the cowardly son of the stage-line's owner Patrick Desmond, namby-pamby Ernie Adams, driver Cactus Mack and café entertainer Bonnie Jean Hartley. Working title was DEVIL'S DEPUTY, referring to Reed who has a terrific windup fistfight

with Johnny Mack.

LAND OF THE LAWLESS (1947 Monogram)

It's a battle of wits and six guns as Johnny Mack Brown turns the tables on claim-jumping owlhoots in one of his better Monogramers. J. Benton Cheney's script has a few twists and surprises as Golden Spur Saloon owner Kansas City Kate (Christine McIntyre) and her cutthroats (gambler partner Tris Coffin, Marshall Reed, Gary Garrett) try to cheat local ranchers and miners like Raymond Hatton, Steve Clark and Cactus Mack out of their profits. When Kate's local gunnies can't deal with Johnny Mack, the vicious lady imports slick gunman I. Stanford Jolley to egg Brown into gunplay. Film contains one of the best brawls of Brown's series as he smashes Tris Coffin. Saloon girl June Harrison gets to sing a spotlight song, "A Gal A Man Loves to Kiss" ala "A Bird In A Gilded Cage". Harrison was a regular in Monogram's Jiggs and Maggie series as their daughter Nora but was heard from no more. Brown is afforded a brief scene to do a couple of his fancy gun tricks.

VALLEY OF FEAR (1947 Monogram)

A Monogram who-done-it worthy of Charlie Chan. Action and plenty of mystery that will keep you guessing. Who is the killer of Johnny Mack Brown's uncle and the man who framed Johnny for helping his late uncle embezzle bank money? There are plenty of suspects — Sheriff Pierce Lyden, rancher Ed Cassidy, his daughter Christine McIntyre, rancher Steve Darrell, Darrell's foreman Ted Adams and banker Tris Coffin. Finally, Johnny and his old pal Raymond Hatton smoke out the real killer. Good location use of both the Monogram (Melody Ranch) town and the Walker (Placeritas) Ranch.

TRIGGERMAN (1948 Monogram)

Mystery surrounds two pieces of a map to stolen loot sought by badman Bill Kennedy. Wells Fargo detective Johnny Mack Brown investigates by hiring on at the ranch run by Virginia Carroll where the loot is buried. Her foreman is Brown's old sidekick Raymond Hatton, but in this one they don't know and are distrustful of each other at first — which gives the film a different flavor. Plenty of action including, with Marshall Reed, one of the best barroom knuckle-busters in the Brown series. Leading lady Virginia Carroll was Mrs. Ralph Byrd. After a long career as a character actress, she's now retired in Santa Barbara.

FRONTIER AGENT (1948 Monogram)

High action content makes this a better than average Johnny Mack Brown as land promoter Kenneth MacDonald and his outlaw ranihans (Dennis Moore, Lane Bradford) want the telegraph to come to their town of Spurlock rather than through Baxter where rancher Ted Adams, his daughter Reno Browne, foreman Raymond Hatton and ranch hand Riley Hill are bringing the line. The outlaws cause plenty of trouble before Brown and his pals bring them gun law justice. Brown is in top form looking great in an untypical black hat and black bib shirt. Watch for Monte Hale's brother Bill as 'Edwards' near the end of the show.

SHERIFF OF MEDICINE BOW (1948 Monogram)

Unusual in that, instead of being an out of town stranger who helps those in need, Johnny Mack Brown lives in and is the sheriff of prosperous Medicine Bow, to which paroled old time bank robber Raymond Hatton returns to see his daughter Evelyn Finley. Their handyman, Max 'Alibi' Terhune (and his dummy Elmer) discovers gold on the ranch but sly badman Bill Kennedy (the banker), Frank LaRue (the assayer), George J. Lewis, Carol Henry, Peter Perkins and Bob Woodward frame the one-time bank robber in an attempt to grab the ranch from Hatton and Finley. Finley, one of the best stuntlady doubles in the business, gets several chances to display her riding ability and expertise with a buckboard. This was Max Terhune's first with Brown. Hatton hung on for two more before Terhune stepped in as Brown's sidekick for five, then the budgets were cut and Brown went a while with no saddle partner at all. Badman Peter Perkins has his best role of the only six westerns he appeared in for '47-'48. After this one he vanished. No telling if he became a plumber in Boise, ID, or a grip in Hollywood. Good J. Benton Cheney script nicely paced by director Lambert Hillyer make this one of the best of the late '40s Brown Monograms.

OVERLAND TRAILS (1948 Monogram)
Johnny Mack Brown dusts off the old Bob Steele plot as he (and pal Raymond Hatton) go after his father's killer. Bill Kennedy and his mob (Pierce Lyden, Holly Bane, Bob Woodward, Boyd Stockman) partnership and grubstake miners, then, if they strike it rich, the gang bumps them off and takes over their full claim 'legally'. A notch above the average Brown from this time period, with several striking plot twists and fine built-in suspense from director Lambert Hillyer. Good support from Virginia Belmont, Virginia Carroll, Steve Darrell and Ted Adams. The script (by prolific Jess Bowers aka Adele Buffington) with its multiple plot elements (which involves a suicide, highly unusual for a B-Western) stretch beyond B confines giving me the idea the story might have been intended for one of those bigger budgeted Monogram/Allied Artists B+ westerns of the period.

HIDDEN DANGER (1948 Monogram)
Plenty of six-gun action in one of the best of the latter day Johnny Mack Brown B-Westerns as he and his two pals, Raymond Hatton and Max 'Alibi' Terhune, expose a crooked Cattleman's Protective Association run by Myron Healey as the brains heavy in the first of his many B-Westerns and TV episodes. Even Healey's niece, Christine Larson, is deceived by her uncle's underhanded ways. Distinctive for a B-Western is the uncommon 'gunman's code' duel between Johnny and hired gunslinger Carol Henry wherein the two opponents know each other and show respect for each other's reputation as a gunman. Both Hatton and Terhune were in three together with Brown, but after this one it was just Terhune for 5 more leaving Johnny with no sidekick to rely on for a while. Brown and Hatton had been a team for 45 westerns since GHOST RIDER in '43.

LAW OF THE PANHANDLE (1950 Monogram)
When Texas bandits loot, rob and terrorize, Marshal Johnny Mack Brown rides hard to enforce the LAW OF THE PANHANDLE. Sheriff Riley Hill can't handle the lawlessness and sends for Marshal Brown. They discover the railroad is coming through and someone is buying up all the ranches in Green Valley to make a nice profit. But who? Is it big land owner Ted Adams? Stage line owner Myron Healey? Telegrapher Milburn Morante? Johnny Mack fights hard to stop the panhandle raiders (Marshall Reed, Lee Roberts, Carol Henry). Jane Adams is Adams' daughter, in love with Sheriff Hill. One of Brown's better latter-day B's filled with gunplay, fights and action. Directed by Lewis Collins. Tris Coffin offers some off-screen narration.

WHISTLING HILLS (1951 Monogram)

Wham-bam and we're off! A stage holdup by gun rannies Marshall Reed and Lee Roberts led by a black caped, whistling ghost rider on the bluff, followed by a doozy of a barroom brawl between Pierce Lyden and Johnny Mack Brown. Stageline owner I. Stanford Jolley and Sheriff Jimmy Ellison are plagued by holdups until Johnny Mack lends a hand to discover the meaning of Spanish Vengeance and a silver whistle. Two girls, Jolley's niece Noel Neill, and beanery operator Pamela Duncan, girlfriend of Sheriff Ellison. Absolute best of the later Brown Monograms with terrific action, a mystery villain and a twist ending. Scripted by Fred Myton from a Jack Lewis story and directed by Derwin Abrahams.

CANYON AMBUSH (1952 Monogram)

Badmen are gunning for undercover government agent Johnny Mack Brown who poses as ineffectual Sheriff Lee Roberts' deputy to stop a series of Wells Fargo robberies by a black clad mystery rider with a Winchester. Your suspects are the Sheriff himself, newspaperwoman Phyllis Coates, attorney Dennis Moore, rancher Russ Whiteman, townsman Pierce Lyden and Wells Fargo agent Hugh Prosser. Later Monogram tight budget shows but still one of the more interesting of Brown's latter-day westerns with plenty of gunplay and a well handled mystery villain angle.

Johnny near the end of his film career.

PHOTO GALLERY

Ed Cassidy, Johnny and Frances Robinson. (Johnny's horse is called Royal.) DESPERATE TRAILS (Universal, 1939).

Johnny with Jack Rockwell (circa 1937). It was recently discovered that Rockwell's name was John Trowbridge - brother of actor Charles Trowbridge.

Anne Gwynne and Johnny in OKLAHOMA FRONTIER (Universal, 1939).

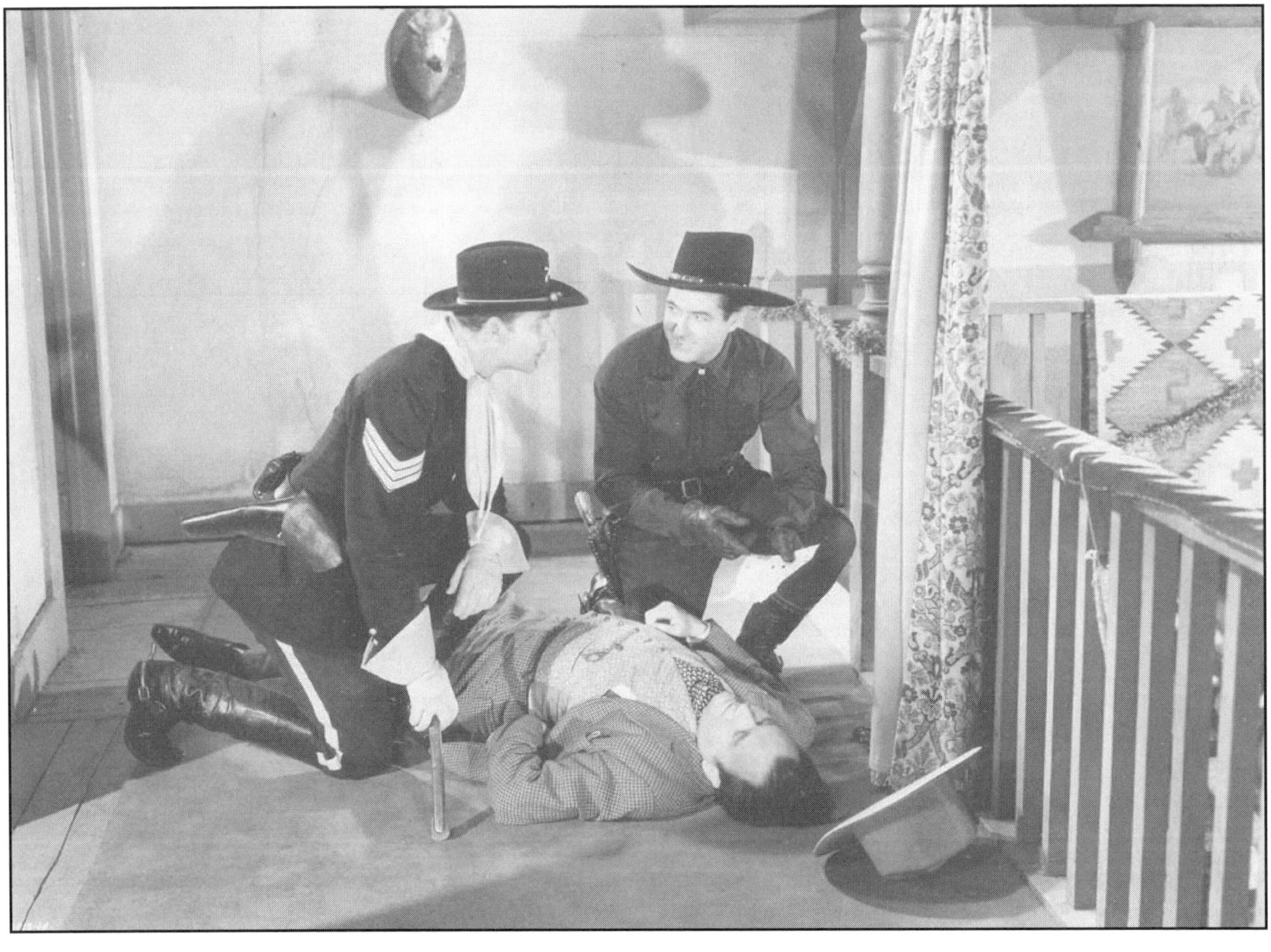

Lane Chandler with Johnny in OKLAHOMA FRONTIER (Universal, 1939).

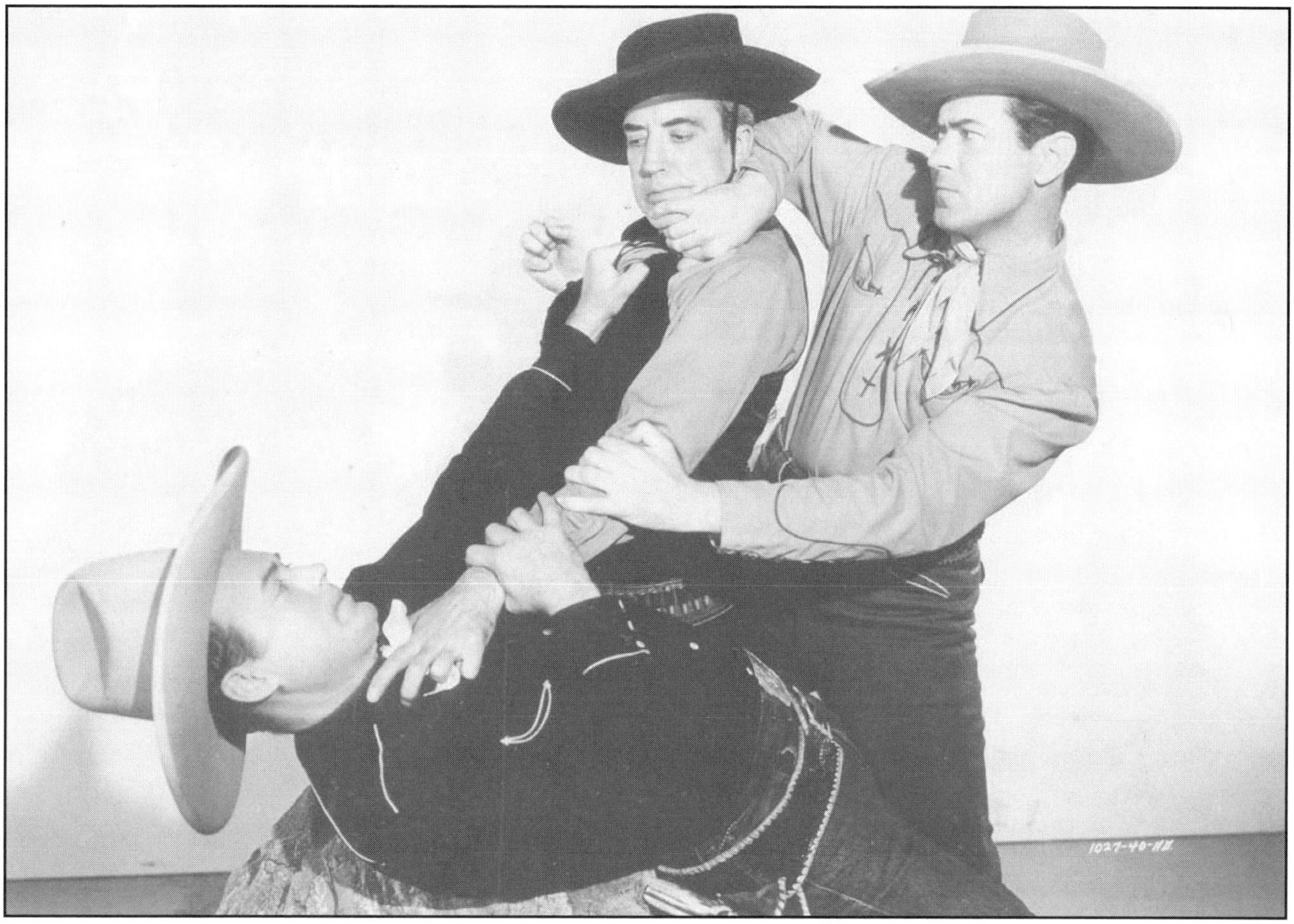

Bob Baker, Ted Adams and Johnny in RIDERS OF PASCO BASIN (Universal, 1939).

Johnny with Louise Stanley in the 15-chapter serial, THE OREGON TRAIL (Universal, 1939).

Johnny and Lynn Merrick in RAGTIME COWBOY JOE (Universal, 1940).

Nell O'Day, Johnny, Dorothy Short, and Tom Chatterton in PONY POST (Universal, 1940).

Nell O'Day, Ed Cassidy, Johnny, Al Bridge, Frank Shannon, and Kathryn Adams in RAWHIDE RANGERS (Universal, 1941).

Pat O'Malley, Jennifer Holt, and Johnny in DEEP IN THE HEART OF TEXAS (Universal, 1942).

Tom London, Fuzzy Knight, Johnny, Tex Ritter, Jennifer Holt, Lane Chandler, and Bud Osborne in TENTING TONIGHT ON THE OLD CAMPGROUND (Universal, 1943).

Lynton Brent, Kermit Maynard and Johnny in THE STRANGER FROM PECOS (Monogram, 1943).

Evelyn Finley and Johnny in GHOST GUNS (Mongram, 1944).

Riley Hill, Jennifer Holt, and Johnny in the THE LOST TRAIL (Monogram, 1945).

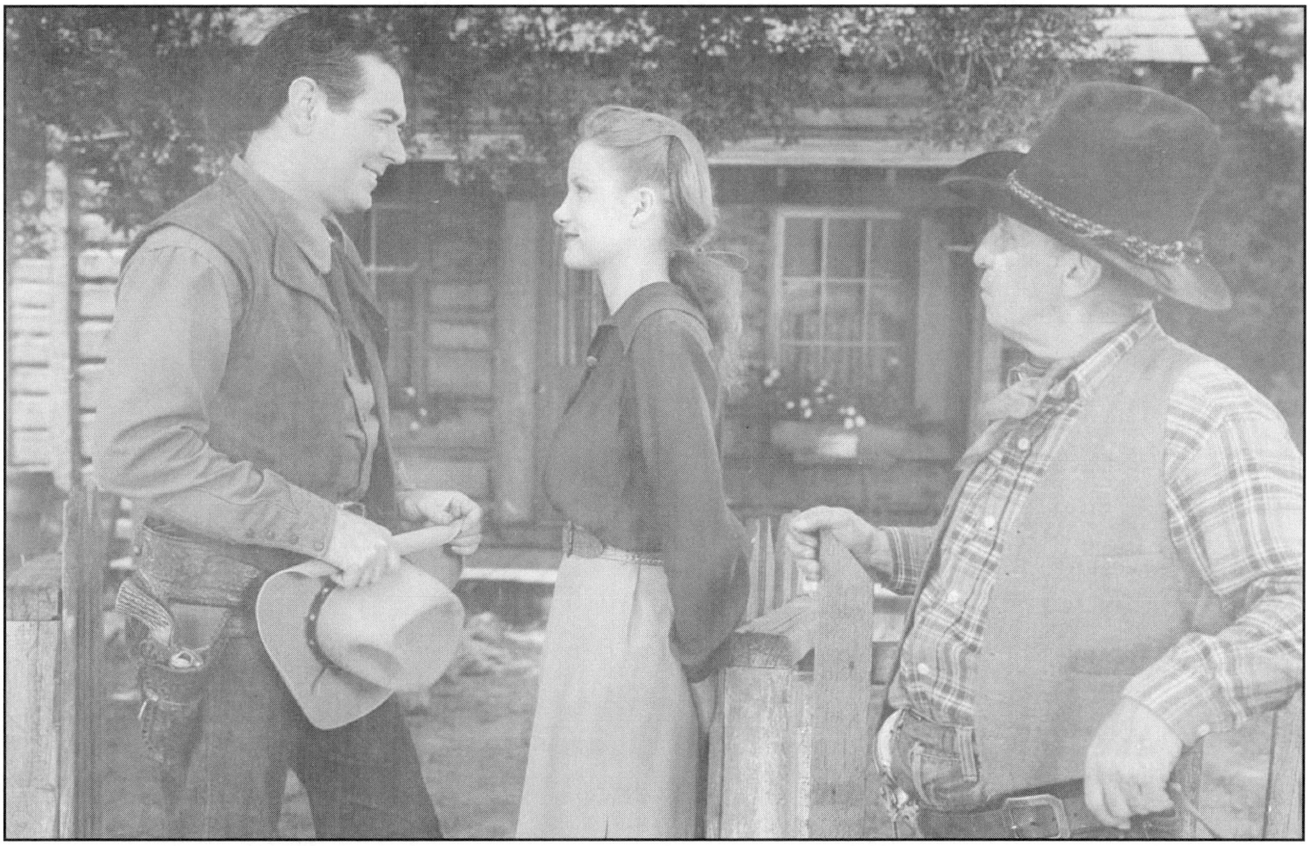

Johnny, Jan Bryant, and Raymond Hatton in SHADOWS ON THE RANGE (Monogram, 1946).

Top left to right: Dick Foran, John Braue, Johnny, Fay Wray, Pat O'Brien, John Wayne, Charles Starrett. Borttom row: Norman McLeod, unknown, Dale Van Sickel, Andy Devine, William Bakewell.

John Merton and Jan Bryant are pictured with Johnny in SHADOWS ON THE RANGE (Monogram, 1946).

Christine McIntyre and Johnny in VALLEY OF FEAR (Monogram, 1947).

Johnny, Lois Hall, Christine McIntyre, and Myron Healey (Monogram, 1951).

Publicity shot of Tex Ritter and Johnny (Universal, 1942).

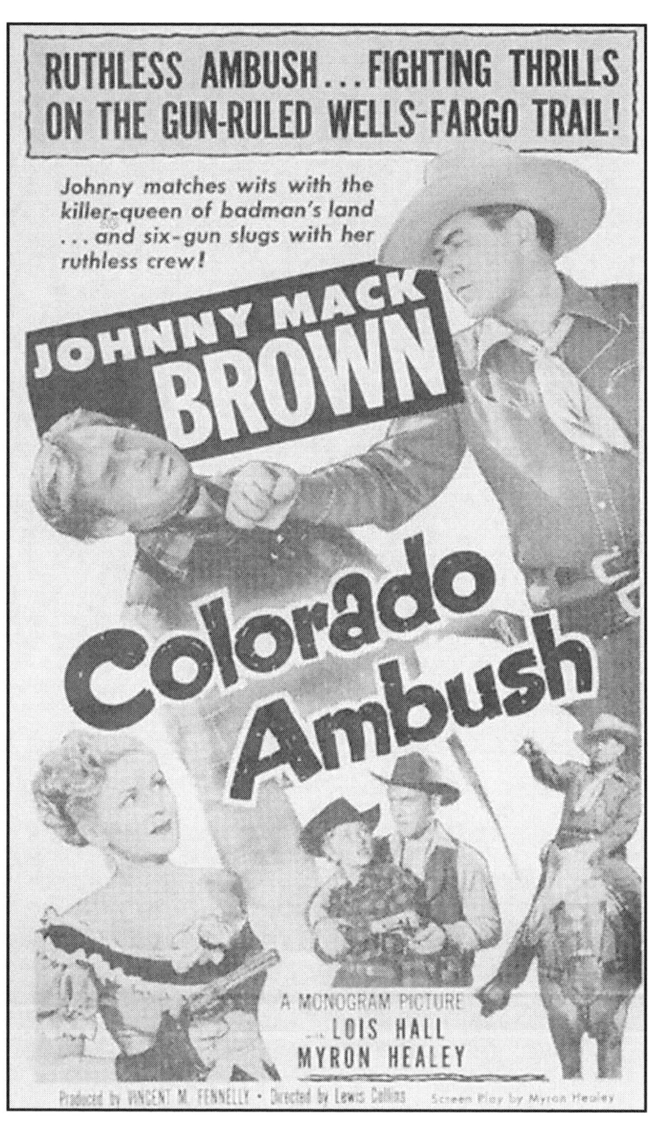

Johnny socks Myron Healy (Monogram, 1951).

Publicity agent, Jewell Smith, watches as Johnny performs some gun tricks.

Virginia Herrick and Johnny in MONTANA DESPERADO (Monogram, 1951).

Johnny meets up with his fans at the Hitching Post theater in Los Angeles (circa 1950).

Johnny with Roy Rogers and Dale Evans (circa 1946).

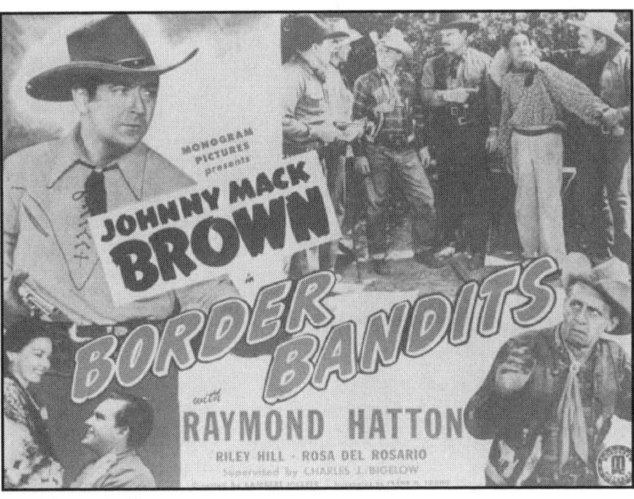

Lobby card from BORDER BANDITS (Monogram, 1946).

Lois Hall looks on as Johnny displays his stag-handled six-shooter.

Johnny tries out his passing arm.

Johnny with Claire Windsor attending a polo match at the Riviera club.

ABOUT THE AUTHOR

Reared in Oak Ridge, Tennessee, Bobby Copeland began going to the Saturday matinee B-Western movies at nearby theaters. He was immediately impressed by the moral code of these films, and has tried to pattern his life after the example set by the cowboy heroes. After graduating from high school and attending Carson-Newman College and the University of Tennessee, he set out to raise a family and start a career at the Oak Ridge National Laboratory. His love for the old Western films was put on the shelf and lay dormant for some 35 years. One Saturday, in the mid-eighties, he happened to turn on his television and the station was showing a Lash LaRue movie. This rekindled his interest. He contacted the TV program's host ("Marshal" Andy Smalls), and was invited to appear on the program. Since that time, Bobby has had some 100 articles published, written nine books, contributed to twelve books, made several speeches, appeared on television over 30 times, and has been interviewed by several newspapers and four independent radio stations as well as the Public Radio Broadcasting System to provide commentary and promote interest in B-Western films. In 1985 he was a co-founder of the Knoxville, Tennessee-based "Riders of the Silver Screen Club," serving five times as president. He initiated and edited the club's newsletter for several years.

In 1996, his first book *Trail Talk* was published by Empire Publishing, Inc. (one of the world's largest publishers of books on Western films and performers) It was followed by *B-Western Boot Hill, Bill Elliott: The Peaceable Man,* and *Roy Barcroft—King of the Badmen,* and *Charlie King—We Called Him Blackie.* In addition to these popular books, Bobby also self-published *The Bob Baker Story*, *The Whip Wilson Story,* and *Five Heroes.* He has attended some 60 Western film festivals, and met many of the Western movie performers. He continues to contribute articles to the various Western magazines, and he is a regular columnist for *Western Clippings*. In 1988, Bobby received the "Buck Jones Rangers Trophy," presented annually to individuals demonstrating consistent dedication to keeping the spirit of the B-Western alive. In 1994, Don Key (Empire Publishing) and Boyd Magers (Video West, Inc. & *Western Clippings*) awarded Bobby the "Buck Rainey Shoot-em-Ups Pioneer Award," which yearly honors a fan who has made significant contributions towards the preservation of interest in the B-Westerns. He will soon be featured on a four-hour DVD about the history of B-Western films.

The author, Bobby Copeland, is pictured in a shirt and pants that belonged to Johnny Mack Brown.

Bobby is an active member at Oak Ridge's Central Baptist Church. He retired in 1996 after 40 years at the same workplace. Bobby plans to continue his church work, write more B-Western articles, and enjoy his retirement with his faithful sidekick, Joan.

More Great Western Books available from Empire Publishing . . .

SILENT HOOFBEATS

by Bobby J. Copeland

A Salute to the Horses and Riders of the Bygone B-Western Era

A beautiful book saluting the great and beautiful horses of the Saturday matinee Westerns! They are all here—Trigger, Champion, Black Jack, Topper and all the rest. Not only is this a book about the horses, but it also contains extensive commentary by the cowboy heroes. And, it is loaded with wonderful photographs.

You will learn many of horses' backgrounds, how they were obtained by the cowboys, and incidents and accidents that happened while filming.

You will also learn which cowboy
...broke his arm when he fell from his horse and had to be replaced by another star.
...cried when his horse died.
...said horses were stupid
...beat his horses until they screamed.
...had his horse buried, instead of stuffed, because it was cheaper.
Plus...many more interesting and revealing items.

TRAIL TALK

by Bobby J. Copeland

Bobby Copeland has become a well-versed Western writer in recent years. His down-to-earth style appeals to most every fan.

*** IT'S A WESTERN STAR QUOTE BOOK ***
Hundreds and Hundreds of Quotes from Your Favorite Cowboys and Cowgirls.

IT'S A WESTERN MOVIE TRIVIA BOOK
You Will Learn...
- What member of TV's "Gunsmoke" was Rex Allen's cousin.
- Who told the studio that the Lone Ranger role was stupid.
- What famous cowboy star divorced his wife and married his mother-in-law.
- Much, much more!

*** IT'S A WESTERN MOVIE HISTORY BOOK ***
- It informs who were the top 10 money makers from 1936-1954.
- The real names of Cowboys & Cowgirls.
- What America meant to John Wayne
- And more!

ONLY
$12.50
(+ $2.00 s/h)

BILL ELLIOTT: The Peaceable Man

by Bobby J. Copeland

*** UNLIKE ANYTHING EVER PRODUCED ON BILL ELLIOTT***

- Wild Bill Elliott
- Bill Elliott in the Comics
- Bill Elliott's Personal Life
- Popularity Ranking of Bill Elliott
- Bill Elliott's Obituary
- They Knew Bill Elliott
- Bill Elliott's Principal Sidekicks
- Bill Elliott and His Horses
- The Real Wild Bill vs. The Reel Wild Bills
- They're Talking about Bill Elliott
- The Starring and Non-Starring Films of Bill Elliott

EMPIRE PUBLISHING, INC. • PO BOX 717 • MADISON, NC 27025 • PH 336-427-5850 • FAX 336-427-7372

B-WESTERN BOOT HILL

A Final Tribute to the Cowboys and Cowgirls Who Rode the Saturday Matinee Movie Range

by Bobby j. Copeland

NEWLY REVISED AND UPDATED! Now includes the obituaries of Rex Allen, Dale Evans, Walter Reed, Clayton Moore, and others. ***You asked for it—now here it is . . . an extensively updated version of B-WESTERN BOOT HILL. (The first printing sold out!) An easy reference guide with hundreds of new entries, updates, and revisions. If you've worn out your original BOOT HILL, or are looking for a more complete B-Western reference book, this is the book for you!***

*** 1000+ ENTRIES ***
The Most Complete List Ever Assembled of Birth Dates, Death Dates, and Real Names of Those Beloved B-Western Performers.

*** IT'S A LITERARY MILESTONE ***
Bobby Copeland has produced a literary milestone which surely will rank at the top among those important Western film history books printed within the past 30 years. *Richard B. Smith, III*

*** OBITUARIES AND BURIAL LOCATIONS ***
Through the years, Bobby Copeland has collected actual obituaries of hundreds of B-Western heroes, heavies, helpers, heroines and sidekicks. Also included is a listing of actual burial locations of many of the stars.

*** MANY PHOTOS THROUGHOUT ***

ROY BARCROFT: King of the Badmen

by Bobby J. Copeland

A WONDERFUL BOOK ABOUT A GREAT CHARACTER ACTOR

In this book, you will find:

- A detailed biography
- Foreword by Monte Hale
- How he selected the name "Roy Barcroft"
- Letters and comments by Roy
- Roy's views about his co-workers
- Co-workers' comments about Roy
- Roy's fans speak out
- Other writers' opinions of Roy Barcraft
- Filmography

CHARLIE KING

We called him "Blackie"

by Bobby J. Copeland

Who was the "baddest" of the badmen?

Many will say it was Charlie King.

This book is a salute to Charles "Blackie" King— one of the premiere B-Western badmen.

Includes:

- The most comprehensive information ever printed on "Blackie"
- The truth about Charlie's death... including his death certificate
- Comments by noted Western film historians
- Remarks by co-workers
- Writers' opinions of Charlie's acting and his career
- Cowboys with whom he worked
- Studios that employed him
- Filmography
- Many photos
- Much, much more

ONLY $15.00 (+ $2.00 s/h)

EMPIRE PUBLISHING, INC. • PO BOX 717 • MADISON, NC 27025 • PH 336-427-5850 • FAX 336-427-7372